The Timothy Principle

Roy Robertson

NAVPRESS
A MINISTRY OF THE NAVIGATORS
P.O. Box 6000, Colorado Springs, Colorado 80934

© 1986 by Roy Robertson
All rights reserved, including translation
Library of Congress Catalog Card Number: 85-62293
ISBN: 0-89109-550-0
15503

Unless otherwise identified, all Scripture quotations in this book are from the *The New King James Version*, © 1979, 1980, 1982, Thomas Nelson, Inc. Publishers. Another version used is *The King James Version* (KJV).

Printed in the United States of America

Contents

Author

Roy Robertson met The Navigators in 1941 in Honolulu the day before the attack on Pearl Harbor, where he was stationed as a Navy pilot. Roy joined Navigator staff in 1945 and lived in the home of Dawson Trotman, the founder of The Navigators. In 1947 Roy opened the Navigator ministry in Texas. In 1948 he became the first Navigator missionary abroad.

Roy was a missionary in China and opened the Navigator work in seven Asian nations. He has served as the Asian director and overseas coordinator for The Navigators. As a Navigator missionary Roy founded and directs an autonomous ministry, Training Evangelistic Leadership.

Roy and his wife, Phyllis, live in Denton, Texas. Two of their children, Janet Lewis and Susan Rice, with their husbands, are Navigator missionaries in Africa.

Preface

Why this book? I feel a godly responsibility to pass on the heritage I have received from my spiritual and physical parents. In my latter years, I have realized the far-reaching impact my parents have had on my life. My dad, a champion golfer, taught me to play the game of life to win. My mom entertained our neighbors and numerous relatives with gracious southern hospitality and loving good deeds. I hope these qualities can be passed on to my children.

But this book is about spiritual reproduction. I have had many teachers, but only one spiritual father (1 Corinthians 4:15). By God's grace and through His unsearchable ways, the man selected to be my spiritual father, to guide me in the paths of righteousness, was Dawson Trotman, founder and first president of The Navigators. But that is another story. I'm not writing about an organization or a man; I'm writing about spiritual parenthood.

My spiritual parent taught me things that made a tremendous difference in my outlook and my spiritual fruitfulness. He enlightened my young mind and heart with principles that were in the Word all along but unseen by me. As I share some of those same principles in this book, I hope they can be the kind of blessing in your life that they have been in mine.

I'm not trying to glorify my parents, spiritual or physical. They had their own prejudices and peculiarities, just as I have. But I think that God wants us to have a basic receptivity to what our parents want to teach us. Scripture tells us, "Remember those . . . who have spoken the word of God to you, whose faith follow, considering the outcome of their conduct" (Hebrews 13:7). We would all do well to follow the guiding ideals of the faith of our spiritual mentors.

In this book I have set forth a thesis, a conviction, as a challenge to Christendom: Spiritual reproduction, as revealed in both the Old and New Testaments, is the vital link for carrying out the Great Commission of Jesus to "go . . . and make disciples of all the nations . . . teaching them to observe all things that I have commanded you" (Matthew 28:19-20).

This process of perpetuating the faith can be accomplished effectively through "the Timothy principle." Just as Paul adopted Timothy to follow in his spiritual footsteps, you can find someone special to be your spiritual child, someone who shares your vision for ministry. As Paul told Timothy, his young apprentice, "My son, be strong in the grace that is in Christ Jesus. And the things that you have heard from me among many witnesses, commit these to faithful men who will be able to teach others also" (2 Timothy 2:1-2). This is the spiritual multiplication process in action—a process that spreads like leaven through the Pauls and Timothys of this world.

1
God's First Two Commandments

I was stranded in Shanghai! It was January 31, 1949. I couldn't find the people who were scheduled to meet me. Because of the confusion on this typical Chinese New Year in pre-Communist mainland China, my ship had berthed at a different pier.

As I stood alone in the most densely packed city of the world, I felt overwhelmed by the sheer jumble of humanity—people everywhere. I had never realized there could be so many people in one place, and this was only one part of one city of a great nation that contained almost a fourth of the world's population.

But that is what I had come for—people. As the first Navigator missionary abroad, I'd come to win the Chinese to Christ and disciple them. I could see right away that I had my work cut out for me, as is the case for any missionary going to a foreign country.

The coolies began grabbing the baggage of the other passengers, pushing a bamboo pole through the handles. They disappeared into the crowd, bellowing at anyone who dared get in their way. While I was pondering what to do, one of the passengers on the ship came to my rescue. I loaded my old canvas sea bag and my battered suitcase onto his vehicle and he drove me to the historic headquarters of the China Inland Mission at 53 Sinza Road. There I remained until I became established on my own.

As I made my way through the crowded streets, fascinated by all these boisterous, jostling, quaintly-dressed, strange-sounding Chinese people, I began thinking about how these masses of humanity got there.

Very simple. They obeyed God's first commandment to Adam and Eve: "Be fruitful and multiply; fill the earth and subdue it; have dominion over the fish of the sea, over the birds of the air, and over every living thing that moves on the earth" (Genesis 1:28). For whatever motivation, the people of the earth obeyed this command and began multiplying. Today's population, approximately five billion people, resulted from their obedience. Some sources estimate that by 2000 A.D. there will be six billion people on earth.

But unless Jesus Christ returns before that date, most of these billions will die without knowing Him. Why? Because Adam disobeyed God's second commandment.

CONSEQUENCES OF DISOBEDIENCE

The second command, a prohibitive "thou shall not," carried a terrible curse if not obeyed. "But of the tree of the knowledge of good and evil you shall not eat, for in the day that you eat of it you shall surely die" (Genesis 2:17).

When Adam disobeyed this order from God, he began the process of death and the sin nature that is passed on to every person. The Apostle Paul confirms this concept in Romans 5:12: "Through one man sin entered the world, and death through sin, and thus death spread to all men." Thus God is not responsible for sin.

Sin is each individual's personal responsibility. It is man's voluntary disobedience and rebellion against God. By definition, sin is the breaking of God's law (1 John 3:4). Paul declares in Romans 1:19-21 that because man is knowingly disobedient to God's authority and law, he has no excuse for his sin. Therefore, each person's sin is *individual, willful,* and *inexcusable.*

Adam's disobedience began a whole process of universal death and destruction. This disobedience marred but did not destroy God's handiwork. Along with the curse, God gave a new promise and hope for a glorious future! He promised that from the seed of woman would come a Savior who would destroy the power of the Devil. The formula of hope is simple and wonderful:

1. Through God, the first man was given physical life (Genesis 2:7).

2. Through Adam, we inherit both our physical life and the seed of death.

3. Through the second Adam, Jesus Christ, we gain eternal life and have victory over death.

THE PRINCIPLES OF PHYSICAL AND SPIRITUAL REPRODUCTION

Though the Fall marred life, it did not destroy life. Life can still be transmitted through the process of reproduction. My thesis is that *God's basic plan for perpetuating life, both physical and spiritual, is through reproduction.*

There are two key principles about reproduction. First, *only life can produce life.* This is obvious in the physical realm. I proposed to my wife on top of Victoria Peak, overlooking the fascinating harbor of Hong Kong. Later we were married at the beautiful mountain estate of Glen Eyrie, Navigator headquarters in Colorado Springs. Eventually we returned overseas. One of our children was born in Colorado and our twins were born in Singapore. Our days for physically producing children are now past, but the seed of life has been passed on to our offspring. We have grandchildren, and there will probably be many more. Even after we die, our children and grandchildren will continue to produce offspring, and their children will produce even more children. The process of physical life will thus go on and on.

Spiritual life begins through Jesus Christ. He is the Life that brings man back from spiritual death (John 11:25, 14:6). When you believe in Christ, the Spirit of God is implanted in your heart. This Spirit confirms your salvation to your own heart and to the hearts of others. Spiritual life begins in Christ and is then passed on to others through the Christian, who possesses spiritual life.

It is our responsibility to pass on this spiritual life to others. They receive Christ through faith in the Word. But how can people believe unless we tell them about Jesus? This question is asked in Romans 10:13-15. God's plan reveals that mere human beings on earth, not the angels of heaven, are the means of bringing other people to Christ.

The second principle is that *everything produces after its own kind.*

While home on furlough in 1954 from my first missionary term in Asia, I attended a conference for pastors held at Glen Eyrie. Dawson Trotman, founder of The Navigators, spoke on the subject of spiritual reproduction. He said, "Dogs produce puppies, cats produce kittens, sheep produce lambs," and he continued to lecture on the facts of animal descent. We knew all about that concept. What we wanted to know was how to reproduce Christians. But Dawson wasn't finished making his point yet.

"Look at this verse," he said excitedly. "I never really saw it until today! This is the heart of the whole matter! 'And God said, "Let the earth bring forth grass, the herb yielding seed, and the fruit tree yielding fruit *after his kind, whose seed is in itself,* upon the earth: and it was so"'" (Genesis 1:11, *King James Version*).

Suddenly I saw it, too, and so did many of the pastors. *God's basic plan for evangelizing the world is through spiritual reproduction!* Every born-again Christian has the wonderful privilege and duty of bringing spiritual life to others. Spiritual life is not transmitted through angels, nor through cold facts and information, nor through special miracles. It is transmitted through *us,* people who are spiritually alive!

God's basic plan is that this spiritual life should be transmitted through believers to reach others. Each of us who knows Jesus as his or her Savior is God's instrument. We are the means through which the gospel flows to another person to give him eternal life. The eternal, incorruptible seed of life everlasting is *in you and me!* Spiritual reproduction is an exciting adventure.

Bearing Spiritual Fruit

How precious is life! How we struggle to hold on to it!

This becomes especially clear when one is faced with death. Twice, as a Navy pilot flying in World War II, I thought I was going to die. One time I saw tracer bullets piercing the fuselage of my plane. The bullets were not fired by the enemy but by my own wingman, who did not see that my plane was directly beneath his as I pulled out of a nearly vertical dive.

Another time while taking off from an aircraft carrier, I sensed, before getting to the end of the deck runway, that my fighter plane lacked the power necessary to become airborne. Desperate, I cut throttle and applied full brakes. My plane stopped a few feet from the edge. As I looked down at the angry sea, I trembled and prayed. Yes, life is precious.

Though life originates with God, it is passed on by us. "Be fruitful and multiply." This first command relates directly to reproducing physical life. But there is also spiritual reproduction. Jesus mentions it in John 15:16: "You did not choose Me, but I chose you and appointed you that you should go and bear fruit, and that your fruit should remain." Fruitbearing is a major theme in the teachings of Christ and of the apostles.

What is fruitbearing? The New Testament refers to fruit in two ways: what you are and what you produce.

FRUITBEARING—WHAT YOU ARE

What are we really like deep inside? We know the answer in two ways: our heart tells us and the Bible tells us. It depends on whether we are controlled by the Spirit or by the flesh. Both bring forth their own types of fruit. The fruit of the Spirit is love, joy, peace, longsuffering, kindness, goodness, faithfulness, gentleness, and self-control (Galatians 5:22-23).

But seed sown in the flesh brings forth awful results. You become what you sow. Paul's partial list of the fruit resulting from yielding to fleshly lusts includes adultery, sexual impurity, idolatry, sorcery, hatred, jealousies, wrath, strife, envy, drunkenness, wild parties, etc. (Galatians 5:19-21).

James explains that sin starts when temptation and lust come together in the womb of the heart (James 1:14-15). Paul says that the fruit of sin is death (Romans 6:21-23). The fruit of the Spirit is life; the fruit of the flesh is death.

Sin generally starts small, but the end result can be devastating. The alcoholic begins with his first drink, the chain-smoker with his first cigarette. Divorces can stem from the first unreconciled quarrel or from that first refusal to forgive one's partner for an offending act.

A person does not fall into the bondage of uncontrollable sinful habits all at once. Rather, it is a step-by-step process. In her book *The Triumph of John and Betty Stam,* Mrs. Howard Taylor traces the "Seven Awful Steps Downward," showing how trifling with sin leads to yielding to sin on a habitual basis, a process that ends with total separation from God.

FRUITBEARING—WHAT YOU PRODUCE

Since everything produces after its kind (Genesis 1:11), *what you are determines what you produce.*

Jesus teaches, "A good tree cannot bear bad fruit, nor can a bad tree bear good fruit" (Matthew 7:18). Bearing good fruit is our duty and destiny.

Our duty—The main purpose of a fruit tree, obviously, is to produce fruit. Jesus tells us to "go and bear fruit" (John 15:16). This is our great duty. This is the Great Commission. It involves obedient action—going into the world as a light into darkness. This command is repeated elsewhere: "Go therefore and make disciples of all the nations . . ." (Matthew 28:19); "Go into all the world and preach the gospel" (Mark 16:15); "and you shall be witnesses to Me in Jerusalem . . . and to the end of the earth" (Acts 1:8). Thus, Christ sends us into the world to witness by life and lip to bring others to Christ.

The fruit of marriage is physical children. If we abide in Jesus, those of us who are mature should produce the fruit of spiritual children. There are indeed exceptions, but our normal God-given function is to reproduce—both in the physical and the spiritual realms.

Our destiny—Jesus said, "I have *chosen* you, and *ordained* you, that ye should go and bring forth fruit" (John 15:16, KJV). This is our destiny. It is God's wonderful plan for populating both earth and heaven.

The early Church Fathers, overly concerned with the consequences of the Fall of man, did not heed many of the commands and promises of God available by faith. Many of the Church Fathers pictured God as arbitrarily foreordaining some people to heaven and some to hell, with man having no part in bringing people to Christ. Augustine went so far as to say that no man could dare assume that he was saved.

But Jesus said, "I have *ordained* you to bring forth

fruit"—fruit unto God, fruit unto eternal life. And His beloved disciple John wrote his Gospel and epistles so that we might know we have eternal life and declare our experience to others, who might then know also.

In his book *The Celebration of Discipline,* Richard Foster challenges us to take part in God's program:

> It is easy for us to be defeated at the outset because we have been taught that everything in the universe is already set, and so things cannot be changed. We may gloomily feel this way, but the Bible does not teach that. The Bible pray-ers prayed as if their prayers could and would make an objective difference. The apostle Paul gladly announced that we are "colaborers with God" (1 Cor. 3:9); that is, we are working with God to determine the outcome of events. It is Stoicism that demands a closed universe, not the Bible. Many with their emphasis upon acquiescence and resignation to the way things are as "the will of God" are actually closer to Epictetus than to Christ. Moses was bold to pray because he believed he could change things, even God's mind. In fact, the Bible stresses so forcefully the openness of our universe that, in an anthropomorphism hard for modern ears, it speaks of God constantly changing His mind in accord with His unchanging love (i.e., Ex. 32:14; Jon. 3:10).[1]

Let's apply this type of "changing prayer" to fruitbearing. Fruitbearing requires prayer. As you believe the promises of God, ask Him to help you go into the world and bring forth spiritual fruit from your own life and witness, thus setting in motion the process of spiritual reproduction.

Notes
1. Richard Foster, *Celebration of Discipline* (San Francisco: Harper & Row, 1978), page 32.

3

Fruitbearing Begins with Discipline

Discipline. We want its results—the sweet honey of victory; the glory and the excellence. Yet we shy away from the pain that is a necessary part of discipline. We look for an easier way.

Lila, our youngest daughter, was a member of her high school's cross-country track team. Because this team easily won first place in competition against all the other international high schools in the Philippines, her school sent a selection of its best runners to the Far East Cross Country Tournament held in Korea. Our girls won first place. But it took discipline—and pain—to achieve the victory.

One day before the trip, Lila commented on the qualities of various runners who were trying to qualify for the trip to Korea. She stated that one girl in particular would probably not make the team. She said, "When we're on the other side of the hill where the coach can't see us, she quits running and starts walking. She's just not willing to suffer the pain."

To achieve spiritual goals also requires pain and disci-

pline. When I was single and living in California, I was ministering to a talented high school senior named Wes. Perhaps I
was giving him more assignments than he was willing to do, for
one day he asked, "How can I get spiritual, real quick?" I said,
"I don't know of any quick way. You must discipline your life.
Growth is slow."

Apparently my answer did not satisfy Wes, for after I went
overseas he asked the same question of others. In fact, he went
all the way to the president of The Navigators, Lorne Sanny, to
get the answer. He asked Lorne, "How do I get spiritual, real
quick?" Lorne said, "Wes, there is no shortcut to spirituality."

No shortcut! Jesus clearly taught this in the famous Upper
Room discourse, when He supped alone with His true disciples
before going to the Cross. John 15 is a key chapter in the Bible
on the doctrine of bearing fruit. Here we find the concepts of
cleansing through pruning and abiding. Pruning involves
pain. Abiding in Christ requires discipline.

PAINFUL PRUNING

"Every branch in me that beareth not fruit he taketh away: and
every branch that beareth fruit, he purgeth it, that it may bring
forth more fruit" (John 15:2, KJV).

What is this purging process? Is it something we do in
order to purify ourselves? Is it something that God does in us?

Eastern religions and philosophies teach that the body is
inherently evil. Some Hindus inflict their bodies with physical
pain in order to drive out sin. Some of the "holy men" walk
barefoot on live coals to demonstrate their holiness. Others lie
with bare backs on a platform of pointed nails or push needles
through their cheeks without drawing blood in order to show
their superior link with the spirit world. The ascetic practices of
the early Christian monks show that some of these ideas
crossed over into the early traditional church.

Even in the Philippines today, certain volunteers pierce their bodies with jagged pieces of glass and metal. They carry heavy crosses through the steamy streets of Manila on "Black Friday" in hopes of placating an angry God from exacting punishment for some fleshly sin of the past.

But purging as taught by Jesus in John 15 is not the vindictive act of an angry God. Nor is it something achieved through the self-inflicted torture of the body in order to drive out sin. Purging is the clipping away of unproductive areas of our life by the loving hands of a compassionate God who wants us to enjoy greater usefulness and blessing. This pruning is God's work. Yes, there is pain involved, but "afterward it yields the peaceable fruit of righteousness" (Hebrews 12:11).

There are many biblical examples of how this trimming process prepares a believer for greater usefulness and blessing. David is one. God anointed him to be king of Israel, but first his heart was purged from ambition and vainglory by having to endure seven years of fugitive existence in the wilderness.

The road to the palace for Joseph was not a paved super-highway. Rather, it was a rough, circuitous route. It led through the "pit," where he was sold by his brothers into slavery. It also led to a difficult detour when Potiphar, the captain of Pharaoh's guard, falsely accused him of making sexual advances on his wife, resulting in Joseph's imprisonment. These difficult events prepared Joseph to eventually become prime minister in the land of Egypt, where he was in a position to help save his people from starvation.

The pruning process is done by God. Only He can direct this delicate operation. But our attitude in the midst of these trials is important. If we rebel against His guidance, chafe under the circumstances of His choosing, or run away from His calling, we will not become a fruitful branch in His vineyard.

David Morken, a missionary leader who formerly directed the Youth for Christ work in Asia, once told his staff, "God is not as much interested in our actions as in our reactions!" How do you react to God's pruning in your life? Your answer is vital.

ABIDING IN CHRIST

The second key to fruitfulness, according to Jesus' teachings in John 15, is a life of daily abiding in Him: "If you abide in Me, and My words abide in you, you will ask what you desire, and it shall be done for you" (John 15:7).

Abiding in Christ is having a continuous fellowship with Him. This is done through prayer and the Word of God. The flesh resents these practices, opposing the spirit that longs to know more about Jesus. Thus it is important to engage in the disciplines of prayer and the Word in order to gain victory over the flesh. Only then can you truly abide in Christ. If you do this faithfully, Jesus says you will produce *much* fruit: "By this My Father is glorified, that you bear much fruit; so you will be My disciples" (John 15:8).

4

Foundations for Spiritual Growth

The early Navigator-trained serviceman was easy to identify, because he always carried with him two black books: a Bible and a devotional notebook. Before Daws Trotman began his work among servicemen, he organized Bible clubs among junior high and teenage students. The boys' groups were called *Dunamis,* the Greek word from which we get our word "dynamite," since the gospel is the dynamite of God. The girls' groups were called by the Greek name *Martures* ("martyrs," or "witnesses"), those willing to lay down their lives for God. These groups were the ones with whom Daws started the disciplines of the quiet time and the spiritual notebook.

The devotional notebook is an important tool in helping a young disciple maintain a disciplined walk before God. As a serviceman I began using Navigator notebook materials. They were a tremendous blessing to me. Today many excellent discipleship notebooks have been developed that can be purchased through various channels. In the following chapters, discipleship principles from the early Navigator notebook materials—principles relevant in any age or cultural context—will be explained and illustrated.

THE QUIET TIME

One of the most important disciplines for abiding in Christ, regardless of your stage of growth, is the practice of a daily quiet time—a time to be alone with God. Though it is simple, it requires great discipline. But it is a vital subsoil of the fruit-bearing life.

The quiet time is a practice of discipline that begins to prepare a disciple for spiritual reproduction.

The person—The quiet time is an opportunity to be alone with God, communicating with Him through prayer. When we pray, we must not forget that God is a person—actually three wonderful persons! Life comes from Him; we are created in His image. We are not communicating with nature, or an abstract force, or some distant phenomenon. We are actually talking with the eternal living God who appeared to Abraham, Isaac, and Jacob, the God who walked and talked with Adam in the cool of the evening.

What makes God even more vivid for us is Jesus Christ, His only begotten Son, who lived on the earth for around thirty-three years. The events of His life—what He did, what He said, how He reacted in various situations—are recorded in the New Testament.

God, through Jesus Christ, lives in us today. God's Spirit also dwells within us, stirring our hearts toward Him. The living God of the universe, the Spirit of truth, wants to fellowship with us. Always remember this when you begin your quiet time (John 4:23-24).

In prayer, simply open your heart and talk to God. He is there—always. We should talk as freely to God as we would to any other person, except that He is more loving, more understanding, more helpful, and more precious than any one else.

The period—The Bible does not confine our quiet time of prayer to a particular time of the day. Daniel observed disciplined prayer at three different times of the day: morning, noon, and evening. He faced a den of lions rather than give up observing his regular prayer times. The psalmist speaks of praising God in prayer seven times a day (Psalm 119:164). Paul tells us to pray without ceasing (1 Thessalonians 5:17).

However, most of us struggle to maintain praying to God regularly for just one period of the day. For most of us, the best opportunity for a *quiet* time is in the morning before breakfast. Some can't do it at that time. My wife, for example, observes her quiet time after she has fed the children and sent them off to school. My regular quiet time is in the morning from 6:00 to 7:00. No one interrupts me—not even my wife or children—during this special period set aside for God.

Some of my Asian friends have their quiet time in the evening. I learned why when I stayed in a village in central Java in the family farmhouse of Pak Purwo, a graduate of the TEL (Training Evangelistic Leadership) program, a ministry that I lead. At 5:00 a.m. the sound from a loudspeaker abruptly awakened me. Though it was still dark, people were shouting, singing, and rushing about with great activity. The noise came from a small coffee shop in the front part of Pak's house where his mother sold coffee and rice cakes to early-rising villagers. It sounded like they were all in my room. In a sense they were, because the farmhouse did not really have rooms—only thin partitions to block off certain areas.

The sheep and pigs had to be fed. Then the children had to be fed and sent to school. At 7:00 a.m., which now seemed like mid-morning, several workmen came in to see Pak Purwo in order to get information for rebuilding a bridge washed out by recent rains.

We rested some in the afternoon, but before nightfall we walked forty-five minutes over a slippery, muddy road to a church. There we had a two-hour Bible study with lay members. We then walked back to his home in the dark, holding a small flashlight to avoid places where the road was flooded. We had supper at 10:00 p.m. By 11:00 I was ready for bed! But this was the time when Pak Purwo reached for his Bible and asked if I would join him in his devotions. He regularly read his Bible and prayed after the rest of the family had gone to bed. Obviously, some people need to have their quiet time in the evening.

Regardless of what period of day you set aside for your quiet time, it is very important to observe it faithfully so that you can grow in your knowledge of Christ and have regular fellowship with the living God.

The place—It helps me to have a place where I can be alone and undisturbed for my quiet time. At home my bedroom is off limits to everyone else until I appear for breakfast. Sometimes I pray and quote verses out loud, which is somewhat embarrassing when others are present. So a private place is important for my personal worship.

When I travel with our gospel team or with other people, I select, during the previous night, the spot where I intend to observe my morning devotions. Sometimes I choose a place outdoors under a tree, or a spot by a fence, or some private nook inside the house. With a little extra effort, I can usually find a place to be alone with God for my quiet time.

For a couple of years I lived at the first Navigator home with the Trotman family, along with eighteen other staff members. With all these people around, it was difficult to find a private spot for my personal devotions. But I found a place. I had to walk for five minutes up the hill in back of the house until I reached a deserted sheep pasture with a magnificent view overlooking the city of Pasadena. I would slip through a break in the barbed wire fence and go to a spot I designated as my private altar to God. Morning by morning, from 6:00 to 7:00, I worshiped God there. I was never interrupted. This spot became the victory field for many a battle waged to maintain progress in my walk with God.

Seven years later when I returned from the mission field, I sought out this place to renew my dedication to my wonderful Lord.

The plan—The overall plan for your quiet time should include a time in the Word, a time for prayer, and a time to write something down. The sequence in which these things are done can vary according to your mood or impressions. You are fellowshiping with a Person. Sometimes you speak; sometimes you listen. Sometimes you may even want to sing! Go ahead.

But don't be vague or dreamy. Try to get something specific out of each encounter with the Lord. Then write it down!

Two excellent aids for developing your quiet time are *Seven Minutes with God* and *Appointment with God,* both published by NavPress, the publishing ministry of The Navigators.

PRAYER LISTS

Dawson Trotman taught his disciples, those who were "navigating for Jesus Christ," to keep a prayer list. In fact, I learned to establish two lists. I still use them today, over forty years later.

The temporary list—The first was called "the temporary list." It was then a printed blue sheet, punched with holes so that it fit into a 3½-by-6-inch notebook. I have changed the size and color of my notebook, but I still keep a temporary list. I have selected some samples of my prayer requests from the past two months. Requests are written on the left, with the answers on the right.

TEMPORARY PRAYER LIST

REQUEST	ANSWER
1. "Same mind and same judgment" (1 Corinthians 1:10) at staff meeting.	1. God gave real unity—above expectations.
2. Make Saut willing and eager to go to the Philippines.	2. Saut responded with ready heart.
3. Our staff too proud—we must humble ourselves.	3. Some have evidenced humility. God spoke to my heart too.
4. Money to buy tickets for trip.	4. 3/8—Still waiting . . . Believe God will supply in time.
5. Bring love and unity between T and L.	5. God worked in both hearts.
6. Help in writing this chapter of this book.	6. My secretary said this chapter was a blessing to her.
7. God's help in giving message to Korean church in Manila.	7. Dave Brougham just called—Mrs. Kim was helped yesterday by my message.
8. Need to reorganize my files. Enthusiasm for mundane tasks.	8. Made *some* progress at least.
9. Finances to come from my letter to Houston donors for India evangelism.	9. God supplied in His ways from Oklahoma, not Houston. Praise God. Pressure lifted.
10. Invitation from churches to hold citywide crusade in Calcutta.	10. 3/15—Still problems, but tentative plan. Lay leaders meet Haggai in November.

The permanent list—The second prayer page we learned to use was yellow. It was for permanent requests. Each person had his own style of arranging it. I found it helpful to divide my regular prayer duties according to the days of the week.

Don't let your permanent list get too complicated. A prayer list should serve as a jog to your memory to give you a good start in prayer. It also helps to keep your mind from wandering off into vague generalities. It should be a joy, not a burden. Keep it simple.

I pray for certain people daily: my wife, mom and dad, my children, and myself. I pray for many other people once a week. I select categories (co-workers, relatives, missionary friends, etc.) and divide the names into sections for prayer Monday through Sunday.

Some things need not fit into a regular prayer list. For

instance, I feel I should pray for all who give to my ministry. My prayer plan for this is to pray for each one as I write a personal note acknowledging my appreciation for his or her gift.

Don't make the list too long, at least not at first. Personally, I like to keep a rather short list and then pray for other people and new situations as God brings them to mind. To keep the list fresh, I revise it and change the order every few months.

Here is a sample of my current permanent prayer list:

PERMANENT PRAYER LIST

	TEL Leadership	Staff	Country	Relatives & Close Friends	TEL Board	Prayer Partners
Mon.	Laurens & Merrie	Sjauri Tanga	India	Nora	Larry & Susan	Dave & Rose
Tue.	Jacob & Martha	Saparman Ephraim	Philip-pines	Aunt Winny	Clay & Betty	Wyatt & Nancy
Wed.	Marv & Sue	Swan Raj	Indonesia	Ron	Jerry & Marchetta	Jim & Nell
Thu.	Dave & Kathy	Simon Pramod	Singapore	Bernie	Bob & Dee	Jack & Jody
Fri.	Bill & Peggy	Joko Kumar	China	Matt	Mal & Barbara	Don & Betty
Sat.	Tanto	Dindo Kumar	Hong Kong		Bob & Rosella	Leon & Virginia
Sun.	Saut & Molly	Elbert	U.S.A.		Ed & Gladys	Steve & Peggy

DAILY PRAYER LIST

1. My wife, Mom, Dad, Sis, children, Mom Hapke, Pohlads
2. Confess my recent sins
3. That God will keep me from sin and help me grow in Christ
4. Help and guidance for the day

THE WORD OF GOD—AN OVERVIEW

As a young Christian serviceman, I was greatly helped by the first message I heard by Daws Trotman. This message focused on how to maintain discipline in the Word of God. The primary thrust was a statement by Jesus: "If ye continue in my word, then are ye my disciples indeed" (John 8:31, KJV).

Although I had been deeply motivated to get into the Word through a group of servicemen who called themselves Navigators, I didn't meet their founder, Daws Trotman, for two years. After graduating from my training in the Naval Air Corps, I became a flight instructor at Corpus Christi, Texas. Several of us on the base helped lead a regular weekly Bible study class that averaged about 125 service personnel. Ensign Jim Farley, who got me started on Navigators materials, invited Daws to spend a few days ministering to our group. I took leave so I could room with Daws in the hotel and drive him to the various meetings we'd arranged.

At the first meeting, Daws gave the illustration of "The Hand" to demonstrate five methods for getting a firm grasp of the Word.

He compared the little finger to *hearing the Bible,* pointing out that the little finger is quite weak. Most of us forget the messages we hear on Sunday mornings. Daws asked if anyone could remember the text and major points of five messages they had heard over the past year. None could. If we grasp the Word with just our little finger (by hearing), Satan can snatch it easily from our grasp. Daws visualized this by asking a sailor to hold the Bible using only his little finger. Daws easily snatched it from him.

The second finger, which he compared to *reading the Bible,* is a little stronger. We retain maybe fifteen percent of what we hear and about forty percent of what we read. So if we hear the Word *and* read it, we will get a stronger grasp on the Bible. But even this isn't strong enough. Daws demonstrated this by quickly snatching the Bible from a sailor who was holding it by the little finger and the adjoining finger.

Then Daws elaborated on the next two stronger fingers.

The third finger, our middle one, represented *Bible study*. Daws asked if we knew the difference between Bible reading and Bible study. One serviceman said that when we read the Scriptures more carefully it becomes Bible study. "No, we should always read the Scriptures carefully," said Daws. Then he explained that Bible study differs from reading by employing pen and paper. To do Bible study we write something down. It has been said that "thoughts disentangle themselves passing over the lips and through the fingertips."

Then he talked about our pointing finger, *Scripture memory*. He felt this was the strongest finger and the means for getting the firmest grasp of the Word of God. Memorizing the Word is the key to victory over sin. Daws claimed he had never heard of anyone who continued to memorize and review Scripture consistently who would then continue to be controlled by gross sins of the flesh. "Either God's Word will keep you from sin, or sin will keep you from God's Word," was a quote that all of us learned.

Through memory we obviously have the strongest grasp on the Word, for we retain one hundred percent of what we properly memorize, whereas we retain fifteen percent from hearing, forty percent from reading, and seventy from studying.

Scripture meditation was compared to the thumb. The thumb cooperates with all the other fingers to provide a firm grasp. Meditation links with all the other methods and strengthens them. When the sailor held the Bible tightly in his hand, squeezing with all fingers, Daws couldn't rip it away from him.

This illustration permanently changed my own concept and methodology in gaining an overall useful knowledge of the Word of God. I adopted lifetime goals and sought to form habits that would give me a meaningful grasp and understanding of God's fathomless Word.

In giving this basic illustration, Daws showed from the Bible how each method is commended and commanded by

God. He also pointed out God's promises to bless each person who would faithfully incorporate these methods into his own lifestyle. These are not the exact verses Daws used in every case (I've made a few revisions from my own studies), but this list will show how God commends, commands, and blesses those who take in the Bible in these five ways:

	COMMENDED	COMMANDED	BLESSING
HEAR	Ezekiel 3:10	Jeremiah 22:29	Luke 11:28
READ	Nehemiah 8:8	1 Timothy 4:13	Revelation 1:3
STUDY	2 Timothy 3:16-17	2 Timothy 2:15	Acts 17:11
MEMORIZE	Psalm 119:11	Deuteronomy 6:6	Psalm 40:8
MEDITATE	Psalm 1:2-3	Joshua 1:8	1 Timothy 4:15

THE WORD OF GOD—HEARING

If we are going to profit from a sermon, we need a hearing aid! Not to help us hear better, but to help us concentrate and remember. So many people get so little out of a sermon. Reason: They don't pay proper attention.

As a boy I entertained myself during the sermon by counting organ pipes or the number of squares on the ceiling. Others think about sports, menus, or the coming week's activities. This is nothing new. Ezekiel complained about the same problem of inattention to God's Word more than 2,500 years ago:

> "So they come to you as people do, they sit before you as My people, and they hear your words, but they do not do them; for with their mouth they show much love, but their hearts pursue their own gain.
>
> Indeed you are to them as a very lovely song of one who has a pleasant voice and can play well on an instrument; for they hear your words, but they do not do them." (Ezekiel 33:31-32)

The basic problem in listening to a sermon improperly involves the heart. Often the heart isn't eager to receive spiritual things. It puts up resistance to the Word of truth because it is not willing to obey the exhortations that come from God. This is why God says, "Receive into your heart all My words that I speak to you, and hear with your ears" (Ezekiel 3:10).

Isn't that the wrong order? Don't we hear something first, then act on the information? Not in spiritual matters—because the heart must first be prepared to receive. Only then will it be able to hear. That is the main trouble with the average listener. His heart is not prepared to hear the Word of God.

Think back. Can you recall a time when God really spoke to your heart during a message? Now think again. Wasn't your heart unusually prepared on that day through some circumstance or experience to receive that particular message?

Have you ever heard of people who grew up in a good church but claim that they never truly heard the gospel in that church? No doubt the essentials of the gospel were preached, but the message just didn't penetrate. Why? Basically because the heart wasn't prepared.

Our first hearing aid: Ask God to open your heart to the message. Ask God to speak to you through your pastor. If God is truly speaking, then we should listen well.

The second hearing aid: Take a pen and notebook with you when you go to church or to a conference meeting so that you can record the highlights of the message. My wife always opens her notebook and begins to write as soon as the speaker begins.

On my last trip to the States, I noticed that the pastor of our local church had inaugurated a new system to help people listen to his messages. He inserted a page in the church bulletin with an outline of his sermon and space for taking notes. The point here is that you will get more out of the sermon as you develop the habit of taking notes.

THE WORD OF GOD—READING

Since I did not have a regular Bible reading plan during the first dozen years of my Christian life, I, like most of my friends, read very little. While in college I dedicated my life to full-time ministry—yet I had never even read through the New Testament. My life was filled with church activity, but not with the Word of God. This is not unusual, for a survey in a leading evangelical seminary disclosed that twenty-five percent of seminary students had never read through the Bible.

There are many Bible reading plans available today.[1] One printed guide takes you through the Bible in five years. But five years to read through the Bible seems like such a glacially slow pace for any disciple who continues in God's Word (John 8:31). Surely the minimum daily Bible reading for a disciple should be at least one chapter, which takes only five minutes a day for even slow readers.

My wife Phyllis reads through the entire Bible every year (three chapters daily and five on Sunday). She has read the whole Bible every year since her conversion.

As a missionary I like to read the Bible in the language of the country where I minister. After my first year in China I formed the habit suggested by a veteran missionary to read in English every morning and in Chinese each evening. One year as a special project I tried to read through the New Testament in three languages. I made it in English and Chinese, but only got about halfway in Japanese. A few years later, while living in Indonesia, I assigned myself the project of reading the New Testament in Indonesian.

Let me urge you not to make the mistake I made in my early years of neglecting to adopt a regular Bible reading plan. Without a plan it is easy to become haphazard. Bible reading programs and plans are published by many church groups and parachurch organizations. Some like to read the Bible straight through from Genesis to Revelation. Others like to skip around, reading portions daily from the Old and New Testaments, or even daily portions from the Gospels and Psalms. Choose an approach that fits your need for a given year.

Notes
1. The Navigators have developed an excellent Bible reading plan that can be obtained from NavPress. It is listed in the Appendix at the back of this book.

Digging into the Word

What is the purpose of all this discipline—in prayer and in the Word? Jesus promises that if you abide with Him in the Word and prayer you will bear *much* fruit. You will become spiritually reproductive. It is especially important to plunge deep into God's Word, for only then can we understand His perspective. We can explore God's Word in depth in three basic ways: study, memorization, and meditation.

BIBLE STUDY

Paul says in 2 Timothy 2:15, "Be diligent to present yourself approved to God, a worker who does not need to be ashamed, rightly dividing the word of truth."

We are workers for the Lord. Work isn't always easy; in fact, it is often hard. Very seldom are Bible studies too difficult for the student. More often than not they are too elementary! They fail to sustain interest and challenge for the sincere student who desires to learn more deeply about God and His Word.

Solomon told his son about digging into the Word for wisdom in Proverbs 2:4: "Seek her as silver, and search for her as for hidden treasures." That kind of searching and seeking takes discipline.

Some Bible studies are specifically designed for brand new believers. These studies carefully lead the fresh disciple step by step, spoon-feeding the Word to someone who is unfamiliar with how to handle it. These kinds of elementary follow-up materials are quite necessary for infants in the faith. But after disciples begin to grow in Christ, they should soon be taught to feed themselves. The basic goal of the early Navigator Bible study program was to teach Christians how to feed themselves the Word of God.

Dawson Trotman once changed a bunch of rowdy boys, who had driven off their former Sunday school teachers, into disciplined little scholars who loved the Word of God and who helped bring scores of other youth to Christ. How? By individual attention. By teaching them how to think and study. By challenging them to learn.

Most people do want to learn. If you can show them how to learn for themselves, giving them the joy of self-discovery and the opportunity to formulate their own ideas on the basis of the unchanging Word of God, you will give them the impetus for a great life-changing adventure.

The most exciting kind of Bible study is the kind you design yourself. I enjoy *discovering* truth (it is like finding the hidden treasures Solomon spoke about) much more than having someone else tell me exactly what I should know and do. As a young serviceman, I was so eager to begin a personalized study that I did only one question-and-answer Bible study booklet. Then I launched out on my own with the various methods Dawson taught us, and I've never stopped. I have never lost the thrill of discovering new truths.

The type of Bible study I'm speaking of is personal and inductive. The Navigators have used various formats for chapter analysis study over the years, designated by such initials as ABC, STS, and Advanced ABC, plus topical and character studies. Yet all these studies have five things in common, elements originally articulated by Lorne Sanny:

ELEMENTS OF PERSONAL BIBLE STUDY

1. *Original investigation*—The conclusions and applications of the truth should be your own observations, not the parroting of conclusions from the lectures or studies of others.
2. *Regular and systematic*—Complete the assigned portion within a given period (usually one week).
3. *Written reproduction*—Restate the scriptural thought in your own words. This is where the personal understanding takes place.
4. *Personal application*—Do not simply note what God said to the Israelites or to the Corinthians, but write down what God is communicating to you. Then go and *do* something about it.
5. *Pass-on-able*—Use a reproducible method of study that is simple and clear enough to pass on to others. This book is about "spiritual reproduction." Once you are grounded in the disciplines of the Christ-centered life, you are going to begin reproducing spiritual fruit. You want to have as many tools that can be passed on to others as possible. Thus you will become gradually equipped as a reproducer.

One of the simplest forms of personal Bible study designed for the new Christian to use on a verse or a short passage of Scripture is called the Point Blank (this was designed many years ago by Daws Trotman). It has four sections:

1. *Point of the passage*—What does it say?
2. *Problem of the passage*—What does it say that I do not understand?
3. *Profit of the passage*—What does it say to me?
4. *Proof of memory*—Write the verse or passage from memory.

Each Point Blank study should be completed within the course of a week or whatever time frame is appropriate for the new disciple. For the *Point* section, you can either summarize the passage in your own words (three to eight words per verse) or write an outline. An example of each is given in the following Point Blank Bible study illustration below, which was done on the familiar passage known as the Great Commission (Matthew 28:18-20).

(1) *Point of the Passage* (Summary):
Promising that He is with us in almighty power, Jesus sends His followers to disciple, baptize, and teach all nations.
Point of the Passage (Outline):
Jesus Unfolds the Great Commission
A. His power
   1. All power in heaven
   2. All power on earth
B. His plan: Go to all nations
   1. Make disciples
   2. Baptize in the name of the triune God
   3. Teach obedience to all God's Word
C. His promise
   1. With us always
   2. With us in every new step of faith
(2) *Problem of the Passage*
Why have Christians been so lax in their response to

Christ's command? Is it possible to fulfill Christ's Great
Commission in our generation?

(3) *Profit of the Passage*

Jesus promises that He will go with me as I venture into
the world to share the gospel and teach His Word. My
nearby world is North Texas State University, where my
children and wife attend. It seems like a rather strange
and frightening world at times, for the campus people are
a generation younger than I, with totally different out-
looks on life. But with God's help, I plan to invade this
world at least one day a week, relying on His Spirit to
open doors of communication as I seek to share Christ
with many people who live in a spiritual void.

(4) *Proof of Memory*

"Then Jesus came and spoke to them, saying, 'All authority has been given to Me in heaven and on earth. Go
therefore and make disciples of all the nations, baptizing
them in the name of the Father and of the Son and of the
Holy Spirit, teaching them to observe all things that I
have commanded you; and lo, I am with you always, even
to the end of the age" (Matthew 28:18-20).

The Point Blank soon evolved into the STS (Search the
Scriptures). It is simple and basic, but gives room for extra
research if you wish. The STS study applies the same questions
as the Point Blank, adding Parallel Passages and dropping
Proof of Memory. STS is often done on an entire chapter of
Scripture.

While in the military I did an STS type study on nearly
every chapter of the New Testament, and I have continued
doing other personalized Bible studies through the years. The
following sample STS study is from *The Navigator Bible Studies Handbook* (pages 52-53), done in a summary format. Many
people prefer to use an outline format instead.

STUDY PASSAGE: 1 John 3:11-24 (14 verses)

POINT OF THE PASSAGE:

We have been taught to love each other. This is one way we can tell if we have eternal life—if our actions are loving and righteous. Of course the world will hate us; that's why Cain killed Abel.

Love is Jesus dying for us, and He is our example. This love demands action on our part, such as meeting our brother's needs. This love is not just words.

Loving actions will lead to peace of mind and a clear conscience, and a clear conscience leads to confidence before God. This confidence assures us of being in God's will and having our prayers answered.

The Holy Spirit reminds us of God's presence with us if we continue to have faith in Jesus, and love others.

PARALLEL PASSAGES:

vs.	Reference	Key Thought
11	John 13:34-35	We are commanded to love.
13	John 15:19	The world hates Christians.
14	John 13:35	Love is the test of new life.
15	Matthew 5:22	Hatred or anger with a brother is as bad as murder.
16	1 Thes. 2:8	We should pour out our lives for our brothers.
17	James 2:15-16	We must meet our brothers' physical needs.
22	Hebrews 13:21	Our lives are to be pleasing in God's sight.
23	John 6:29	We are commanded to believe in Jesus.
24	Romans 8:9	The Holy Spirit is proof of God's presence.

PROBLEMS OF THE PASSAGE:

vs. Question

13 Why does the world hate us?

18 Can we also truly express love with our speech?

20 What does it mean for our hearts to condemn us?
    When do our hearts condemn us?

22 How do I really determine what is pleasing in God's
    sight?

PROFIT OF THE PASSAGE:

Verses 18 and 19 say that our confidence and assurance depend on our obedience to God's command to love others in deed and truth. My many anxious moments and doubts are therefore directly traceable to my lack of giving and doing for others.

I intend within the next week to give an entire evening to my children to do "their thing," and one night to my wife at her favorite restaurant.

SCRIPTURE MEMORY

Once I asked Dawson Trotman during a follow-up workshop, "How long do you wait before you start the new convert on a Scripture memory program?" Daws glared at me for a moment, then replied, "Do you mean 'how many minutes' or 'how many seconds'?"

Since its early history, The Navigator organization has emphasized Scripture memory as a vital element—which had been previously neglected—in the process of helping new spiritual babes grow into maturity. In order to help those who had just made decisions to believe in Christ as their personal Savior, Dawson designed a small memory packet with helpful suggestions for beginning a new way of life in Christ. Printed during the early years of World War II when many vital staples like butter, sugar, and gasoline were rationed, the packet was first called the "Bible Rations" or "B Rations." "This is like a bottle of milk to keep a spiritual babe from starving," said Trotman.

Charles E. Fuller used this booklet to follow up the thousands who came to Christ through his radio preaching on the Old Fashioned Revival Hour. Later, Billy Graham asked The Navigators to develop counseling and follow-up materials for his crusades, so this packet was given to everyone who came forward for counseling.

However, when the B Rations were introduced to the crusade committee in England, the British complained that they were tired of rationing after all the war years. So the name was changed to *Beginning with Christ,* which is the present title.

One evening while driving home from a meeting with servicemen in the San Diego area, Daws shared with those of us in the car the story of what led to the development of this simple follow-up material that was eventually used by millions of people. He told us that he and a few of his key men used to hold evangelistic meetings at the National Guard Armory in Los Angeles. Daws would speak, and the team with him would counsel with the servicemen who responded.

Daws was training his men how to be spiritual reproducers. At the end of the evangelistic meetings they would single out servicemen, counseling and praying individually with these spiritual babes for about half an hour. On the way home, Daws would ask his men what they had shared with the converts. Nearly all of them had stressed a verse or two on assurance of salvation, and then a passage on how to get victory over the attacks of Satan. Then each man pointed out to the new Christian what he should do if he falls into sin—how to ask for forgiveness. Each shared a verse on the need to pray about everything.

As a result of this discussion, they all agreed it would be helpful to have a booklet with appropriate verses to memorize and with brief explanations of those verses for fresh converts. Such a booklet was necessary for situations with limited time follow-up.

"Satan fought the printing of this memory packet more than anything else we ever did," Daws said. First, they experienced great difficulty in getting everything together for printing. Then the print shop burned down, destroying all the plates. Work began again. It took a total of eight months to complete the project. Similar unusual difficulties were experienced later when The Navigators were preparing the memory system in Chinese.

Although there has been some revision, the B Rations still retain four verses for giving the new believer assurance in four vital areas:

1. Assurance of salvation (John 5:24).
2. Assurance of victory over sin (1 Corinthians 10:13).
3. Assurance of forgiveness (1 John 1:9).
4. Assurance of provision through prayer (John 16:24).

It is far easier to start a new Christian on Scripture memory than the older Christian, who seems to resist memorizing verses. So start a new convert, whether old or young, on Scripture memory at the outset. Parents should begin helping their children to memorize; it will benefit them all the days of their lives.

However, there is hope for *anyone* to begin the habit of Scripture memory if that person is properly motivated and shown how to do it. Usually the habit of Scripture memory is passed from person to person. If you know someone who is enthusiastic about it, have that person help you begin.

The Navigators have several memory plans. The basic one, called the *Topical Memory System* (*TMS*), is available in most Christian bookstores.

Issue Nine of the *Discipleship Journal*, published by Nav-Press, presents excellent articles emphasizing Scripture memory. In one of the articles, Francis Cosgrove lists fifteen reasons for memorizing the Word of God: increasing our faith, victory over sin, inner cleansing, knowing Bible doctrine, guidance, prayer, Bible study, finding passages, meditation, experiencing the Holy Spirit, worship, not wasting time, counseling, witnessing, and teaching.

BIBLE MEDITATION

As a young missionary in China and Japan I served under David Morken, the director of Youth for Christ in Asia, who was a gifted evangelist and an inspirational Bible teacher. When certain members of Dave's staff complained about his lack of organizational ability, Dick Hillis (who later established Overseas Crusades, now a worldwide mission named O.C. Ministries) took me aside to give me his analysis.

"God is blessing Dave because he is meditating on the Word night and day. In fact, God has promised to make him prosperous." Dick continued in his self-effacing manner to suggest that Dave was wiser than his critics because he meditated so much on the Word, whereas those like himself, who had majored in getting things done, were not so wise or blessed. Dick was not only humble, but correct. I observed that he was also powerful at challenging lives because of his own rich insight into the Word of God.

God surely did prosper the ministry of Dave Morken. The Word flowed from his lips with power and authority. Japanese people bowed publicly in the streets to repent; Chinese people streamed forward in great numbers to believe. Missionaries sometimes wept as they heard the Word preached by this godly man. I overheard a veteran missionary say that he received greater blessing from hearing Dave Morken *merely quote* the

Scripture than by listening to most other people preach.

Dave would tackle a whole book of the Bible, memorizing it in total. Then he would meditate upon it when he reviewed it from memory each day. During the first month in Shanghai prior to the Communist takeover, I accompanied Dave on a business errand down to the "bund," the business center by the Whangpoo River.

As we crowded into a street car, which had standing room only, Dave surprised me by saying, "Let me quote to you the book of Romans." In the midst of the noise, the clanging of bells, and the shouting of the conductor as the street car slowly progressed through Shanghai traffic, Dave calmly quoted about half of the book. We reached our destination before he could finish.

Later he memorized John, Hebrews, Philippians, and other books. He would review the entire book daily and literally meditate upon it night and day in the midst of other chores and obligations. No wonder God mightily prospered his ministry! It is as Joshua 1:8 says: "This Book of the Law shall not depart from your mouth, but you shall meditate in it day and night, that you may observe to do according to all that is written in it. For then you will make your way prosperous, and then you will have good success."

Many have pointed out that the pressures of our present modern lifestyle make it difficult to meditate. According to Richard Foster, the devil is sidetracking our contemporary society by using three major devices: "noise, hurry, and crowds."[1] Yet this may be largely an excuse for our own lack of discipline, because Jesus and His disciples certainly moved in the midst of crowds and noise wherever they went. Certainly Jesus accomplished the great goals of His ministry in an incredibly short period of time. So the answer must lie in our inward spirit more than in our outward circumstances.

The Bible is full of exhortations to withdraw from worldly

distractions in order to wait on the Lord (Psalm 27:14), to consider the heavens, which are the handiwork of God (Psalm 8:3), to count the numerous blessings of God (Psalm 139:18), to search the heart in order to expose wicked thoughts (Psalm 139:23), to talk about God's Word throughout the day (Deuteronomy 6:6-7), and to meditate on the Word (Psalm 1:2-3; Psalm 119:97).

The important thing is to discipline ourselves to meditate in spite of our busy schedule. We should determine to observe a specific quiet time for prayer and meditation in the Word. As we develop habits of meditation during this time alone with God, we will find it easier to recall things from Scripture during the activities of the day (Deuteronomy 6:7).

I have found it helpful to coordinate my reading, memory, and meditation programs each morning into one devotional package. I am now reading through the book of Exodus. Each morning in my quiet time I read, memorize, and meditate on a passage from Exodus, and then I write in my devotional diary a brief Bible study on what God has impressed on me from that passage. I also review all the Exodus verses I have previously memorized up to the part I'm reading that day. Then I meditate and pray over those verses and matters that God brings to my attention.

I don't do these things in this precise order, for my devotional time varies according to the day. Yet I do seek to coordinate my reading, meditation, and memory review during my quiet time. I do not do message preparation and weekly Bible study assignments as part of the quiet time.

Many people will need to adjust their programs according to their work situations. For instance, when I travel, which is about a third of the time, I have much time for Scripture memory and review, but less time for Bible study. So I try to use for meditation those hours that I spend traveling by train, bus, or car.

Although discipline seems difficult and tedious, we need to persevere in faith so that God will make us fruitful. This is the reason for digging into the Scriptures in study, memorization, and meditation. "And let us not grow weary while doing good, for in due season we shall reap if we do not lose heart" (Galatians 6:9).

Notes
1. Richard Foster, *Celebration of Discipline,* page 13.

The Joy of Soul-winning

I moved my family to the Philippines in 1977 to coordinate counseling and follow-up for the Metro Manila Billy Graham Crusade. For six months, day and night, crusade activities absorbed me. "I've never seen you work so hard in my life," my wife told me.

We trained over 4,000 counselors in seventy-two locations using three languages. We developed 1,600 qualified nurture group leaders to hold classes for those who made decisions, particularly to instruct those of Catholic background. We organized a Co-labor Corps of Filipino friends, led by Navigator international trainee Len McGrane, who was assigned to help in this project. Len and his Filipino friends worked round the clock for two weeks processing 22,512 decision slips, sending each name and address to the proper pastor and nurture group leader.

Henry Holley worked even harder than the rest of us. He has no peer in his ability to set up large cooperative crusades in foreign cultures. During one long day of incessant activity, someone asked him, "Henry, what drives you to work so diligently and enthusiastically?" He replied, "When I see the huge crowd gather to hear Dr. Graham preach I receive my first joy, and when I see great numbers come forward in response to the invitation I get an even greater joy."

What a thrill it is to see thousands of people coming to Christ in public evangelism. But what about one-to-one evangelism? Have you experienced that inexpressible joy of leading another person to Christ?

I was first challenged to do this as a teenager by one of my closest friends, Tom Truett. One day Tom, who was the outstanding speaker on our interscholastic debating team and also my personal ideal, confided in me, "The greatest thrill in all the earth is leading a soul to Christ!" Quite a statement! "You mean, greater than being in love with a girl?" I thought in my teenage way.

Although very active in church affairs, I let a number of years slip by before I prayed individually with someone who invited Jesus Christ to come into his heart. By then I was a young flying officer in the U.S. Navy.

One rainy night in 1943, I picked up a hitchhiking serviceman in my old 1938 Plymouth. He saw by the wings on my uniform that I was a pilot, so he began to talk about a recent plane crash near the air base in which a number of people had been killed.

"Aren't you afraid to die?" he asked.

"No, I'm not," I said. "If my plane goes down, my soul goes up."

Then I began to quote the verses which Navigators had taught me regarding the plan of salvation. It was dark and I was driving, so I quoted from memory, giving only a few words of explanation between verses.

After the sixth verse, which was on the need to believe in

Jesus and receive Him into one's heart in order to become a child of God (John 1:12), I paused. "Shall I ask him to receive Christ now?" I thought. My heart raced and thumped so hard I thought he could hear it, but I blurted out, "Will you, in faith, pray right now to ask Jesus to come into your heart?"

As I wondered what his reply would be, I mentally tried to think of a verse to refute his argument. To my surprise he answered a simple *yes.* I stopped the car, and he prayed for Christ to come into his life and save his soul.

Leading that person to Christ was even more thrilling than putting my dive bomber into a vertical dive and pulling out just above sea level. Once I experienced the great joy of soul-winning, I wanted to tell others about their need to be saved. That week I prayed individually with three more servicemen who asked the Lord to save them from their sin and give them the gift of everlasting life.

Forty years later I am a missionary by profession. Since the time of that first incident, I have prayed individually with many people, sometimes in an Asian language, who have invited Christ to come into their hearts. I have been involved in the counseling of hundreds of evangelistic meetings conducted by both foreign and national evangelists.

Does it ever become stale or old? Never! At the time of decision, no matter how tired I may be, I can feel my pulse quicken and my heart beat faster. Heaven and hell lock in combat. God's Spirit penetrates into darkened hearts. I never lose the joy of experiencing the contact with God and eternity that takes place as a person is clearly being born again before my eyes. The change of expression, the light in the eyes, the glow in the face of a newborn spiritual babe makes my heart leap with joy. And not just *my* heart: Jesus says, "Likewise, I say to you, there is joy in the presence of the angels of God over one sinner who repents" (Luke 15:10).

To reproduce life is one of the great joys of our earthly

existence. In the first chapter we noted that God's first and basic command to mankind is to be fruitful and multiply physically. Throughout all history the birth of a child has been cause for great rejoicing and the barren womb has been considered a personal misfortune. In the second chapter we examined Jesus' teaching to show that His disciples have been chosen and appointed to reproduce spiritually. He who bears spiritual fruit becomes a joyful disciple. "These things I have spoken to you, that My joy may remain in you, and that your joy may be full" (John 15:11).

No wonder the reward given by a loving Father to those who bring others into His family is called "our crown of rejoicing"! (1 Thessalonians 2:19).

THE WISDOM OF SOUL-WINNING

Some are quick to say that soul-winning is not *our* responsibility but that it is the work of the Holy Spirit. True, no one is born to new life in Christ except by the Holy Spirit, as Jesus explained to Nicodemus (John 3:3-6). But the priceless privilege of being the messenger of the good news is ours. Where does the Bible say that this work is done by anyone other than the Lord's disciples? "Go *ye* into all the world, and preach the gospel to every creature" (Mark 16:15, KJV). The Bible clearly commands *us* to do this wonderful work. Of course, Jesus promises that He will be with us and that the Holy Spirit will guide us as we share the truth of the gospel.

Others might say, "Yes, we are to do the witnessing, but we have no part in the conversion of a soul." Again the Scriptures indicate otherwise. In fact, the Apostle James closes his epistle with this exhortation: "Let him know that he who turns a sinner from the error of his way will save a soul from death and cover a multitude of sins" (James 5:20). Proverbs 11:30 puts it even more plainly: "He who wins souls is wise."

Why is it wise to spend of our best creative time in an effort to win souls? Let us find the answer by studying the Scriptures.

Old Testament passages—God has promised to heap great rewards on those who turn people away from sin into the path of righteousness. "Those who are wise shall shine like the brightness of the firmament, and those who turn many to righteousness like the stars forever and ever" (Daniel 12:3). On the other hand, if we do not open our mouths to warn others, then we are guilty of serious neglect. God's words of warning are strong (see Ezekiel 3:17-21 and Proverbs 24:11-12). If you do not warn the wicked, they will indeed die in their sin, but their blood shall be on your hands.

Teachings of Paul—The Apostle Paul urged the Ephesian Christians to redeem the time "because the days are evil," and to walk wisely as a testimony of spiritual light before those who live in darkness (Ephesians 5:8-16). He prodded the Corinthian believers to wake up and start proclaiming the reality of the resurrection to people who had an inadequate knowledge of God. Paul blamed this sad circumstance on the carnality of the Corinthian church (see 1 Corinthians 15).

Teachings of Jesus—The multitudes wanted to make Jesus their king because He fed their stomachs with plenty of fish and bread. Jesus told them that they were working for the wrong thing. "Do not labor for the food which perishes, but for the food which endures to everlasting life, which the Son of Man will give you" (John 6:27).

The lesson is this: Don't spend all your effort taking care of the body, for the body will die anyway. Spend your time on nourishing that which will live forever—your soul.

THE VALUE OF ONE SOUL

Sometimes I hear criticism about the large amount of money being spent in evangelistic crusades. My reply is generally,

"Yes, it does take a lot of money. But something of great value is being accomplished. Souls come to Christ, people who will live for eternity in His wonderful presence."

What is the value of one soul? A hundred dollars? A thousand dollars? A hundred thousand? Perhaps it depends on whose soul we are talking about. If it is someone in a far-off, hard-to-pronounce foreign country, some critics may not place the value very high. That is wrong thinking. *Every* soul is of *great* value. Jesus said, "For what is a man profited if he gains the whole world, and loses his own soul? Or what will a man give in exchange for his soul?" (Matthew 16:26). In other words, *one soul is worth more than the whole world!*

"God so loved the world that He gave His only begotten Son, that whoever believes in Him should not perish but have everlasting life" (John 3:16). God sacrificed His own Son to redeem every precious soul.

It is wise for us to examine our expenditure of time. How much of our labor is directed toward taking care of the body? How much time do we spend on that which relates to the soul? How much effort and time do we spend on seeking to win souls to Christ?

Spiritual reproduction *begins* with the joy of leading someone to Christ. But how do we explain the gospel? What do we say? The next chapter gives helpful suggestions on how to explain the essence of the gospel message to someone else.

The Bridge
to Life

Leading someone to Christ is an inexpressible joy. But how is it done? There are some basic elements of presenting the gospel that everyone should know. A very helpful tool, used internationally, is the Bridge illustration. Before explaining how to use it, let me describe how the Bridge came into existence.

THE HISTORY OF THE BRIDGE ILLUSTRATION

During his early ministry, Dawson Trotman taught his Sunday school class of junior high boys to present the gospel by using the following set of verses:
1. The fact of sin—Romans 3:23
2. The penalty of sin—Romans 6:23
3. Judgment is certain.—Hebrews 9:27
4. Christ paid the penalty.—Romans 5:8
5. Salvation is a free gift.—Ephesians 2:8-9
6. You must accept Christ.—John 1:12.

At the same time Daws designed a ladder index for the boys' New Testaments so that they could turn quickly from one verse to another in presenting the gospel to friends. To protect their Testaments, which they carried in their hip pockets, each boy would put his small Bible in a Prince Albert tobacco tin!

In my Navy days, we used Daws's same sequence of six passages, but by then there was a seventh point. This was the assurance of salvation, with John 5:24 as the key reference.

Later, while I was working in Asia, we thought of combining Daws's logical sequence of verses with a dramatic poster used by China Inland Mission workers in order to present God's plan of salvation to people who knew little of the gospel message. The poster pictured many people traveling down a broad road that ended abruptly at a cliff. Their hands reached frantically upward trying to escape the burning abyss at the foot of the cliff, into which they were tumbling.

However, there was also a Cross at the edge of the cliff. A few people turned and, using the Cross, went on to an upward path that led to heaven. Chinese evangelists certainly know how to paint vivid pictures of heaven and hell!

This combination became the Bridge illustration, and fit in well with the Chinese culture, which requires a mediator for all important transactions. The Chinese transact marriages and buy property through a *pao jen,* or a "go-between." Jesus Christ is the go-between for the sinner to get to God. Gradually, after refinements, we had a workable "bridge" that clearly explained the gospel. Others used it, making modifications to fit their way of presenting Christ. As a tool, the Bridge can be used in many forms, each suiting the individual user, giving liberty and power to the presentation of salvation.

HOW TO USE THE BRIDGE ILLUSTRATION

Here is one way to use the Bridge in explaining the gospel:

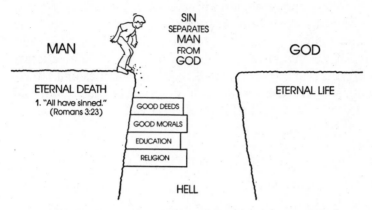

1. In this first picture we see that man is separated from God. Originally, God and man had fellowship together in the garden of Eden. Then Adam and Eve both sinned and were separated from God's presence. The Bible teaches in the first three chapters of Romans that all men, whether born in a Hindu family or born in a Christian family, have sinned. "For all have sinned and fall short of the glory of God" (Romans 3:23).

Man desperately tries to build his own bridges to heaven. Man's most common attempt is through his own good works. But our good works are like filthy rags in the sight of our holy God (Isaiah 64:6).

Some people try to reach God through ethics or good morals. But no one can live up to even his own standard of values, much less to God's standard of righteousness. Man is not able to keep the Ten Commandments, which are the fundamental laws of God. The problem lies in man's deceitful heart (Jeremiah 17:9).

Nor is education the answer. Knowledge simply increases our feeling of guilt. God does not excuse our sin merely because we have been taught the truth. "For not the hearers of the law are just in the sight of God, but the doers of the law will be justified" (Romans 2:13).

"But surely religion will save us," some will say. No, not even religion will bring us back into fellowship with the living God. Religion is good; it offers good advice. Religion tells us what we should and should not do. But religion, whether Hindu, Islam, Jewish, Catholic, or Protestant, cannot forgive our sins and save our souls. Only God can do that. Sinful man does not need more religion. He needs a Savior.

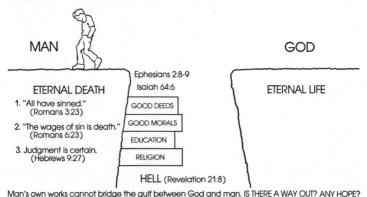

MAN

GOD

ETERNAL DEATH

Ephesians 2:8-9
Isaiah 64:6

ETERNAL LIFE

1. "All have sinned."
   (Romans 3:23)

GOOD DEEDS

2. "The wages of sin is death."
   (Romans 6:23)

GOOD MORALS

EDUCATION

3. Judgment is certain.
   (Hebrews 9:27)

RELIGION

HELL (Revelation 21:8)

Man's own works cannot bridge the gulf between God and man. IS THERE A WAY OUT? ANY HOPE?

2. Not only have all people sinned, but the result of their sin is death. "For the wages of sin is death" (Romans 6:23). Man was not created to die but to live in fellowship with God. Yet because of Adam's sin, man inherits death. And that is not all. The Bible tells us that "it is appointed for men to die once, but after this the judgment" (Hebrews 9:27). Judgment is certain; it is inevitable. Every person is judged by the Almighty God, and those whose sins are not forgiven are eventually sent to hell, a place originally prepared for Satan and his demons (Matthew 25:41).

It is a terrible picture. Alone we cannot bridge the gap to heaven. Left to our own devices we are helpless—cut off from God and condemned by our own sins. Sin . . . death . . . judgment . . . hell. Our spiritual condition is utterly hopeless (Ephesians 2:12).

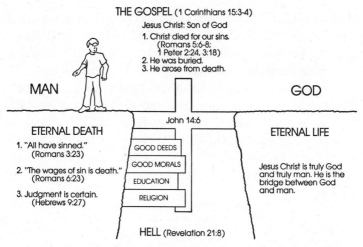

THE GOSPEL (1 Corinthians 15:3-4)

Jesus Christ: Son of God

1. Christ died for our sins.
   (Romans 5:6-8;
   1 Peter 2:24, 3:18)
2. He was buried.
3. He arose from death.

MAN

GOD

John 14:6

ETERNAL DEATH

1. "All have sinned."
   (Romans 3:23)

2. "The wages of sin is death."
   (Romans 6:23)

3. Judgment is certain.
   (Hebrews 9:27)

ETERNAL LIFE

GOOD DEEDS

GOOD MORALS

EDUCATION

RELIGION

Jesus Christ is truly God
and truly man. He is the
bridge between God
and man.

HELL (Revelation 21:8)

3. But God in His great love provided a way of deliverance. He had a wonderful plan, designed before the world began, to bring sons and daughters back to live with Him forever. Only one person could bridge the gap of sin that separated man from God. And that person had to be both man and God. If he was not man, he could not represent us; if he was not God, he could not save us. So God sent His only Son, Jesus Christ, to be born as a man. Jesus is the Son of Man born of Mary, and the Son of God conceived through the Holy Spirit. He is not part man and part God, but one hundred percent man and one hundred percent God. In theological terms, He is called "very God and very man." There is but one person qualified to become our Savior: the Lord Jesus Christ.

This man Jesus did many wonderful miracles, but we are not saved by the miracles. He taught many beautiful lessons, but we are not saved by following the ethical teachings of Jesus. He healed many from sickness, but the healing of the body does not heal the soul. The fact is that we are not saved through all those marvelous things Jesus did during His three years of ministry. The life of Jesus demonstrated that He was the Son of God. But this fact alone was not enough; more was necessary for salvation. Jesus Christ had to die on the Cross for our sins. He died for you . . . and for me. The Cross of Christ is the bridge for us to cross over from death to eternal life.

Yet Jesus Christ not only died to pay for our sins; He arose from the grave so that we might be made righteous (Romans 4:25) and might live forever as children of God. This is the good news, the historic gospel: "that Christ died for our sins according to the Scriptures, and that He was buried, and that He rose again the third day according to the Scriptures" (1 Corinthians 15:3-4).

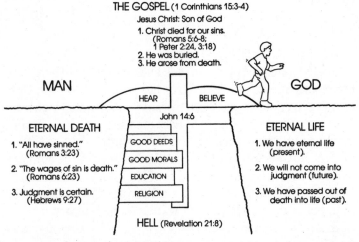

THE GOSPEL (1 Corinthians 15:3-4)

Jesus Christ: Son of God

1. Christ died for our sins.
   (Romans 5:6-8;
   1 Peter 2:24, 3:18)
2. He was buried.
3. He arose from death.

MAN

HEAR   BELIEVE

John 14:6

ETERNAL DEATH

1. "All have sinned."
   (Romans 3:23)

2. "The wages of sin is death."
   (Romans 6:23)

3. Judgment is certain.
   (Hebrews 9:27)

GOOD DEEDS
GOOD MORALS
EDUCATION
RELIGION

GOD

ETERNAL LIFE

1. We have eternal life
   (present).

2. We will not come into
   judgment (future).

3. We have passed out of
   death into life (past).

HELL (Revelation 21:8)

4. Jesus died to save all men, yet all men are not saved. Why? Because God does not force anyone to believe. Each person has a choice, and that choice will determine one's eternal destiny. How, then, can one be saved?

Jesus said, "Most assuredly, I say to you, he who hears My word and believes in Him who sent Me has everlasting life, and shall not come into judgment, but has passed from death into life" (John 5:24).

At this point in your explanation of the Bridge illustration, it is appropriate for you to make a personal challenge to the unbeliever. The following paragraphs are an example of what you might want to say to the person who needs to cross the bridge to Christ:

> Since you have already heard the words of Jesus, you must only believe in order to possess everlasting life. Believe what? Believe that Jesus died on the Cross for your sins, and that He was buried and arose from the dead. Believe that the Lord Jesus Christ is truly the Son of God, and receive Him in your heart as your personal Savior.
>
> Are you willing to believe now? As soon as you do this, you have everlasting life. You will not be judged by God in the future and sent to hell, because all your sins of the past, present, and future have been forgiven by God and covered by the blood of Jesus that was shed on the Cross. You have already passed from death to life.
>
> Jesus says, "Behold, I stand at the door and knock" (Revelation 3:20). Jesus knocks at the door of your heart. Only *you* can open your heart. Won't you open your heart right now and call on the Lord in a prayer of faith? Pray in your own words something like this: "Dear Father in heaven, I believe that Jesus died on the Cross for my sins. I pray that Jesus will come into my heart. Forgive my sins and give me life everlasting. Amen."
>
> To everyone who calls on the Lord in true faith for salvation, God gives the eternal life He has promised. All who are willing to believe will be saved. If you are still lost, it is because you love your sins more than you love Jesus, and thus you are not willing to believe. If you have believed in Jesus, then rest in hope and peace, because He will bring every one of His children into heaven.

Raising Spiritual Children

My wife and I have six children. Indeed, it is an unspeakable joy when our children grow up wisely in both the physical and spiritual realms. The Apostle John said, "I have no greater joy than to hear that my children walk in truth" (3 John 4). In an earlier epistle he wrote a similar thought: "I rejoiced greatly that I have found some of your children walking in truth, as we received commandment from the Father" (2 John 4).

FOLLOW-UP

During the two years I lived in Dawson Trotman's home and the following years, I served directly under his leadership. At that time I heard much about a concept that was being overlooked by most Christian groups as they carried out their regular programs. Daws called the concept "follow-up," and he talked about it constantly.

I had not heard this term used before in church circles. In

fact, to my knowledge the term does not occur in any theological work written prior to World War II. But Daws taught it as the principle of "follow-up" with great vigor.

Most of what I write in this chapter, in fact, most of this book, is an adaptation of the ideas that were committed to me on many occasions by Daws (2 Timothy 2:2), ideas that have been reinforced by the varied experiences and trials through which God has graciously led me.

Follow-up may be defined as *the process of bringing a babe in Christ into spiritual maturity.* Note that it is a process. Salvation is an act. In a split second one can pass from death to life through faith in Jesus Christ, being born again at a certain point in time. But the follow-up process takes considerable time and repetition. Growth in both physical and spiritual life is painfully slow.

Daws often explained, "It takes twenty minutes to a couple of hours to lead a soul to Christ, but it takes six months to a couple of years to bring someone into spiritual maturity." By spiritual maturity, Daws meant more than the ability to survive; he felt that the mature Christian should become a spiritual parent, bearing the responsibility of helping someone else become mature in Christ. This is spiritual reproduction.

TWO TYPES OF FOLLOW-UP

There are two basic types of follow-up: *pastoral* and *personal* (or parental).

Pastoral follow-up is done mostly through the local church. The Lord has given His church pastors and teachers the responsibility of feeding and caring for the congregation.

The Lord emphasized this to Peter when He dined with His key disciples by the Sea of Galilee after His resurrection: "Simon, son of Jonah, do you love Me?" Jesus asked this question three times, and three times Peter answered, "Yes."

Then three times the Lord solemnly told Peter to *feed My sheep* (John 21:15-17).

The thrust of the passage does not lie in the fine shade of distinction in the interpretation of two Greek words used for love: *phileo* and *agapao*. The main lesson is loud and clear: "Feed My sheep!" First the Lord got Peter's attention; then He underscored the importance of follow-up.

In the Upper Room discourse recorded in John 14-16, Jesus pointed out five times that the proof of our love for Him lies in our obedience to His commandments (John 14:15, 14:21, 14:23, 15:10, and 15:14).

"Feed My sheep!" Nourish them in loving care through the Word of God.

Peter never forgot this vivid lesson. At the end of his life, he exhorted his fellow elders, "Shepherd the flock of God which is among you . . . willingly, not . . . as being lords over those entrusted to you, but being examples to the flock" (1 Peter 5:2-3). Peter went on to announce that a "crown of glory" awaits every pastor and teacher who is faithful in feeding the flock (1 Peter 5:4). A pastoral type of follow-up is thus vital for Christian growth.

Personal follow-up is also essential, for spiritual training should take place in the home as well as in the church. Fortunate, indeed, is the young convert who has not only a godly pastor but also a spiritual parent to help him. The pastor must serve many people; he has only limited time for the individual. So the whole Body of the Church needs to be involved in follow-up. Each mature Christian, each true disciple of Jesus, man or woman, should perform the function of either an exhorting father (1 Thessalonians 2:11) or a nurturing mother (1 Thessalonians 2:7).

Jesus has called all His true disciples to glorify God by bringing forth fruit that *remains* (John 15:8,16). We have seen in the previous chapters that this means spiritual reproduction—helping others become mature and fruitful.

This is not just abstract theory or dormant spiritual truth, for it calls for action. I have accepted my parental responsibility of raising up the six physical children God has given me. I have also taken seriously the privilege of being a spiritual parent to certain individuals the Lord has brought into my life. Some of these I adopted because I led them to Christ; others I adopted because the Lord put into my heart a special interest and the recognition that they needed help.

FOUR WAYS TO FOLLOW UP

There are four basic ways to follow up. These are mentioned by Paul in his first letter to the Thessalonians: prayer, personal contact, pen, and proxy.

1. *Prayer*—Paul told the Thessalonians that he prayed night and day that they would become mature in their faith (1 Thessalonians 3:10). Billy Graham has stated publicly that successful city wide crusades can be attributed largely to the concentration of the prayers of thousands of committed Christians toward the conversion and follow-up of souls in a particular area for a particular time.

In any evangelistic program, those who respond should be prayed for name by name. The gospel may be preached to thousands at a time, but people come to Christ one by one. Each soul is precious in the sight of God.

2. *Personal contact*—Prayer and a personal visit should go hand in hand. Paul expressed his fervent desire to the Thessalonians, "praying exceedingly that we may see your face and perfect what is lacking in your faith" (1 Thessalonians 3:10). To the Romans Paul expressed his disappointment in not being able to visit them on previous occasions (Romans 1:10-13). Similar remarks occur in Paul's letters to Corinth, Philippi, and Colosse.

In the crusades sponsored by TEL (Training Evangelistic Leadership) in Asia, we endeavor to maintain extended personal contact with everyone who comes forward to make a decision for Christ.

First, each inquirer is assigned to a counselor who takes thirty minutes or so to explain the plan of salvation using the Bridge illustration as a basic pattern. At the close of this time, there is individual prayer. The counselor prays for the seeker by name. Then the seeker is encouraged to pray out loud in his own words a prayer of faith in the Lord Jesus Christ, whom he receives into his heart as his personal Savior.

Within a week we also try to visit the home of each person who has recorded a decision for Christ, especially any person who comes from a nonChristian background. In TEL crusades each inquirer is assigned to a particular local church, according to previously arranged guidelines. The TEL staff workers offer their services to help train the members of a given church in a visitation program for new believers.

In one crusade in northern Japan, the members of a local church visited fifty-five inquirers from a Buddhist background. Forty-four of these responded by attending, for the first time, one of the local services of that church. People do respond when visited face-to-face, especially when they are shown love and concern.

3. *Pen*—The pen can supplement personal visits. Most of the New Testament epistles were, in reality, follow-up letters addressed to assemblies of new believers. Paul communicated by letter as he traveled from city to city, and even continued his correspondence when he was in prison.

In our Asian ministry we mail a Bible study to every inquirer and recommend a Scripture memory course. This is done by personal contact *and* correspondence. A Japanese man was converted while doing Navigator Bible studies in prison. He sent each completed lesson to our office. We would correct it, and then send back more lessons. A couple of years later he suddenly showed up at my house, needing a place to stay. A jailbird who couldn't be trusted? No, a Christian brother redeemed by grace!

I received him into my Japanese-style home with sliding paper doors that were never locked. He became a trusted member of our household. I gave him a job at our office grading the same type of Bible studies he used to mail in and going out to witness in prisons and gospel meetings. In time he fell in love with and married a dedicated Japanese co-worker. They established a home that has become a splendid testimony to the grace of God. Brother Tsuchiya, a deacon in the church and a trophy of grace, is a fruit of Bible studies done by correspondence—the *pen* method of follow-up.

4. *Proxy*—The first three methods just mentioned are the best means of follow-up. But sometimes we are faced with a lack of both time and the right circumstances, making it virtually impossible for us to follow up directly on all the people who have been brought to our attention. Therefore, I sometimes call on a personal friend to aid in the task. This is follow-up by proxy.

Paul asked Philemon to take back and aid Onesimus, his runaway slave whom Paul had led to Christ. Philemon followed up in Paul's stead. When Paul could not visit with believers in Corinth and Ephesus, he sent Timothy in his place (1 Corinthians 4:17, 1 Timothy 1:3). Similarly, he sent Tychicus to Colosse (Colossians 4:7) and left Titus in Crete (Titus 1:5). In 1 Thessalonians we learn that Paul sent for Timothy, his proxy, to discover how the Thessalonians were doing in their growth in faith.

I endeavor to follow up each individual who crosses my path and makes some kind of new commitment to Christ—by *personal* contact, *pen, prayer* or *proxy*.

The aged Apostle John reminds us, "I have no greater joy

than to hear that my children walk in truth" (3 John 4). This should be *our* joy as well—to see that our spiritual children are sustained in the faith.

Elementary
Follow-Up

Since the most effective method of discipling is the one-on-one method, let's lay out a basic program for one-on-one follow-up and discipling, which can be done in a scheduled weekly meeting with your spiritual babe in Christ.

In the physical family, parents support their baby as he or she learns certain necessary functions—eating, sitting, walking, talking, and so on. Later on, the more complicated aspects of life are taught. But what are the primary needs of a *spiritual* babe in Christ?

TRAINING A DISCIPLE

Assurance of salvation—Don't take for granted the salvation of any disciple. When I arrived in China in 1949, I was introduced to Hans Wilhelm, son of German missionaries who worked for the China Inland Mission (now Overseas Missionary Fellowship). I began to disciple eighteen-year-old Hans. He was a brilliant student and the leader of the youth fellowship. He had memorized the book of Philippians and he regularly spent personal prayer time with Bishop Frank Houghton, the revered General Director of the China Inland Mission.

Where was I to begin in the personal discipling of Hans? According to my general practice, I began with the assurance of salvation. After a time of explanation from the Scriptures, I was amazed at Hans's response: "You know, I have never really been sure of my personal salvation."

"Let's pray right now and make these things certain," I said. We prayed together, and he made certain his personal salvation.

When I'm meeting with a person I've previously led to the Lord, I ask him to explain to me the plan of salvation using the Bridge illustration as a basis. The student should always give back *in his own words* what he has been taught.

John Milton Gregory's classic book *The Seven Laws of Teaching* gives the four steps of learning:

(1) The teacher presents the material.

(2) The student repeats in his own words what he has been taught.

(3) The student uses the information and gives it to some- one else.

(4) The student absorbs it into his daily life.

Growth in the Word—Many Bible teachers concentrate on giving Bible lectures to their students. Daws Trotman's philos- ophy was, "If I can teach a person how to get into the Bible for himself, then I will have done far more for him than if I merely gave him a lecture from the Bible."

Regarding food, the goal of the parent is to teach his child how to feed himself. And this should be the chief goal for the discipler: to teach the young Christian how to feed on the Word of God for himself. How is this done?

In the first week of follow-up, start the new disciple on

Scripture memorization. I recommend that every spiritual babe be given the first packet of Navigators memory materials, *Beginning with Christ.* In time he should be challenged and guided into a lifelong program of Scripture memory, meditation, and review. During your first session, assign the new disciple at least two verses to memorize before you meet together the next week.

In our TEL ministry in Asia, we give new Christians a simple question-and-answer Bible study based on the Gospel of John. This study follows the plan of salvation as given in the Bridge illustration. Thus the student gets a review of the gospel, reinforcing the assurance of his salvation.

Excellent Bible studies for new Christians are now available. I am including a reference to a study from the Gospel of John in the Appendix of this book. It is a series of four leaflets that are given one at a time as each section is completed.

Quiet time—It has been said, "Through prayer I speak to God, and through the Word God speaks to me." Both are vitally important. Early in your regular meetings with a new disciple teach him how to have a quiet time.

The disciples of Jesus said, "Lord, teach us to pray, as John also taught his disciples" (Luke 11:1). We, too, teach disciples how to pray; we teach them how to have a quiet time. (See the material in Chapter 4 on the quiet time.)

One of the best ways to teach someone how to have a quiet time is to do it together. This is the "with Him" principle of Mark 3:14: "[Jesus] appointed twelve, that they might be with Him." Early in your relationship meet together in a special session to have a quiet time together. Pick a time that is suitable to both of you. Don't pressure him into having it the same time you do. (Remember, the *when* isn't sacred.) Then lead him through a quiet time.

Show the disciple how to pray and how to read God's Word. For me, Bible reading is part of my morning devotions, but Bible study is done at another scheduled time. Encourage him to begin reading the Scriptures systematically. The Bible reading chart listed in the Appendix is a useful tool for accomplishing this.

Every disciple should be encouraged to keep a prayer list as an aid in making his prayer time more balanced and specific. Teach the new disciple to thank the Lord for His gracious provision and to intercede for the needs of others, not just to pray for his own immediate needs.

Fellowship with a congregation—As soon as a person receives Christ, he should be linked to a group of believers for his spiritual protection, guidance, and growth. The one-on-one discipling you are doing with him does not replace the fellowship of the Church, though it does serve as an encouragement to be with individual believers in the Body of Christ. Just as the wise parent sends his child gradually to church, to school, and to work in his chosen profession, so the wise discipler doesn't try to teach his spiritual child everything at once. On the contrary, he helps him link effectively with a local church body that will provide stability and spiritual blessing.

In your training, teach your disciple how to take notes as the pastor preaches and how to respond obediently to the messages he hears from the Word of God.

Challenge toward reproduction—Here and now is where the next generation of spiritual reproduction will begin. As you continue your relationship with a disciple, train him not only to learn to do all you teach him but also to begin to share these truths with another person. The thrust of one-to-one time should be reproduction. Keep each principle you teach clear and simple enough so that the young Christian can then teach it to an even newer disciple. Reproduce. "And the things that you have heard from me among many witnesses, commit these to faithful men who will be able to teach others also" (2 Timothy 2:2).

THE USE OF WRITTEN TOOLS IN DISCIPLING

Some carefully selected materials will encourage your disciple to be more consistent in his daily walk with God. Don't try to give him too many choices or options. Remember, he is a spiritual babe. In the early stages you make the choice for him. Keep it simple! In fact, I recommend that you explain only one new portion of materials at a time.

These materials are like tools in the hands of a master craftsman. The end product depends more on the skill of the workman than on the tools he uses.

Not only should you introduce one written tool at a time, but also you should require your disciple to complete an assignment in it before the following meeting. Here is a recommended sequence for introducing new types of materials, with four phases that could vary from a week to several months per phase, depending on the rate of progress of the disciple:

First phase—Introduce the *Beginning with Christ* Scripture memory series. Assign at least two verses to memorize. In this session, you will also have gone over the Bridge illustration.

Second phase—Introduce question-and-answer Bible study material. Continue to memorize new verses.

Third phase—Give your disciple a discipleship notebook. Assign prayer pages. Continue to do a Bible study, and memorize new verses.

Fourth phase—Assign daily Bible reading using the chart in the discipleship notebook. Continue to use prayer pages daily. Do a weekly Bible study, and continue to memorize new verses.

SAMPLE MATERIALS

Here is a consolidated list of written materials to use with the new disciple as basic tools of follow-up:

A. *Beginning with Christ* memory packet

B. Bible studies on the Gospel of John

   1. Salvation

   2. God's protection and love

   3. Devotional life

   4. Outreach

C. Notebook materials—The suggested notebook is very simple. Start with only the necessary pages in order to get the disciple going in some of the basic elements of the Christian life. The three segments of the notebook will be Devotional, Organizational, and Development.

   1. *Devotional*

      a. Prayer pages

        (i) Immediate requests

        (ii) Intercessory prayers for people and missions

      b. Bible reading chart

      c. Quiet time notes

   2. *Organizational*

      a. NOW page (a do list)

      b. Planning page (weekly)

      c. Monthly schedule

      d. Finance page (optional)

   3. *Development*

      a. Sermon notes

      b. Bible study

      c. Scripture memory page

      d. Idea page (optional)

10

Teaching Spiritual Reproduction

THE THREE P'S

If you plan to disciple someone, then you need to agree to meet an hour every week at a scheduled time and place. Discipling is hard enough when done on a regular basis, so I find that to try to disciple someone haphazardly in my spare time and his spare time is a rather futile activity for both of us. If you mean business, then you need to stick to your schedule on a weekly basis.

How do you spend this prime hour of time together? I like to have clear objectives and a general teaching program in mind for the meetings. At the same time it is important to try to keep a relaxed, flexible atmosphere.

There are three basic elements that should be present in one-on-one discipling—"the three P's." The first P is the immediate *personal* things that need a word of encouragement. Generally, you should begin with a time to pray and share how things are going (not too long—maybe about ten

79

minutes). I try to avoid getting too deeply involved in a particular problem in the early stages of the disciple's growth into maturity. His first real need is to grow in the basics of Christian living, thus laying a foundation for solving those deeper problems later by applying the Word of God.

Then I check on the second P: his *progress* on Bible study assignments, quiet time, and Scripture memory. This may take from five to ten minutes.

The heart of the one-on-one time is the third P: a teaching program on the *principles* of discipleship. Each week I present a foundational lesson on one aspect of discipleship. The order and time frame are flexible, but this is my general pattern in the hour with a new disciple:

Personal	10 minutes
Progress	10 minutes
Principles	40 minutes

A SYLLABUS

After receiving my wings in 1942 at the Corpus Christi Naval Air Base in Texas, I expected to be sent out immediately to the Pacific fleet to fight the Japanese, who at that time had air superiority. However, while engaged in the fitness program I suffered a freak accident in which I dislocated my shoulder. It kept me grounded at the base hospital, while the other new pilots of our group were rushed out to the war.

Most likely this freak accident saved my life, for our group suffered heavy casualties in the Coral Sea and in other early battles. I was told that only two of the original sixteen from my class were active at the close of the war.

For the next two years I stayed in Corpus Christi teaching cadets how to fly airplanes. The heart of the cadet training program was one-on-one instruction. It had to be. The airplane had only two seats: one for the instructor and one for the student. Certain cadets were assigned to me for the entire course. It was my duty to teach my cadets how to fly under combat conditions. My skill in teaching a cadet and his skill in applying those lessons could mean the difference between life and death in aerial combat.

Each senior pilot trained young pilots according to an overall syllabus divided into six stages. At the end of each stage my student would be tested. If he received the *up* check from another pilot, he passed. If he received a *down* check in some area, he had to repeat that stage of training. A couple of down checks would generally "wash out" a cadet from flying school.

The syllabus was a guide to help us train pilots effectively. Each flight instructor was allowed a certain amount of liberty in how to train his student, but the most basic task was to prepare him for the test to come. The trainee's first major test was to fly solo. There was no need to teach him complicated maneuvers until he learned the more simple tasks of how to take off and land safely. In the same way, when teaching a disciple I want to discover first if he knows that he is saved and understands the basic plan of redemption. We need not tackle complicated theological problems until he understands the fundamental things of salvation.

This analogy can be carried further in broad simple terms. A young Christian must be taught early how to feed on the Word and how to have a quiet time in order to have strength to cope with the ordinary pressures of life. He must be taught how to have victory over sin through the twists and turns and subtle temptations of the Devil—the kind of maneuvering similar to the controlling of a plane at any given position. The new disciple must be prepared to fight the enemy and rescue souls through evangelism. He should know the importance of "formation flying" with his local church and other Christian groups. He should be ready to do some "instrument flying" as well, venturing out in faith, trusting the promises of God.

This rough analogy holds true only in broad terms, but it was helpful to me as I switched from training pilots for flying combat to training disciples to reproduce for Christ. Combining these military ideas with the Wheel illustration, I developed a syllabus for training people to reproduce in their spiritual lives. I have used this syllabus for many years in one-on-one discipleship. You may want to alter it or perhaps work out your own syllabus. It is very helpful to have a clear outline of your teaching program, whatever it may be—helpful for you and helpful for your disciple as he tries to teach someone else. You will find this teaching plan and syllabus in the Appendix at the back of this book.

THE WHEEL

The Wheel illustration, designed by Dawson Trotman and modified slightly over the years, portrays the requisites of a victorious, Spirit-filled Christian life. The Wheel presents the basics—the *absolutely* essential, *irreplaceable* dimensions for maintaining spiritual health and growth.

The Lord Jesus, using the teaching about the vine, described what is absolutely necessary for fruitfulness in one's life. "I am the vine," Jesus told His disciples. "You are the branches. He who abides in Me, and I in him, bears much fruit" (John 15:5). The Christian *must* abide in Christ to be fruitful.

When Trotman was working with junior high youth, he tried to devise an illustration that would make this vine-branch truth more vivid to his active young audience. A common illustration at the time was that of a three-legged stool with the Word, prayer, and witnessing as the legs. But Daws didn't want to compare the Christian life to sitting on a stool. He wanted something that moved. A wheel!

Jesus Christ is the hub, the center, the driving power of the Wheel of the Christian life. The Christian, as the rim, is vitally connected to Christ through the spokes, but the Word, prayer, and witnessing (as the three components in the stool) were not quite enough; something was missing. Daws felt that the fundamental weakness in the lives of most Christians was their lack of obedience. The rim of the Wheel contains this element: "the *obedient* Christian in action."

The vertical spokes represent our spiritual intake—the Christian's communion with God as he abides in Christ. Through *the Word* God speaks to the Christian; through *prayer* the Christian speaks to God.

The horizontal spokes represent our outreach to others through *fellowship* and *witnessing*—serving the Body of Christ and witnessing to the world for whom Christ died.

11

Spiritual Grandchildren

The power of spiritual reproduction is staggering! If you had twelve spiritual children and each of them produced twelve offspring and each offspring did the same for a total of five generations, you would have 248,832 spiritual descendants.

This tells us the mathematics of spiritual reproduction—the quantity. But how do you qualitatively influence your spiritual descendants? Where do you start? There are two primary considerations: setting the right pace and recognizing the uniqueness of each disciple.

PACESETTING

Most parents wisely observe that their children copy what they do, not what they say. Actions make the deepest impression on a child.

A pacesetter is a runner who helps the other runners keep a steady stride. Spiritually speaking, we often run along with someone else to encourage him in the race of life, to help him keep a steady pace.

This principle permeates Scripture. Jesus told His disciples, "Follow Me, and I will make you fishers of men" (Matthew 4:19). Paul exhorted the carnal, quarrelsome Corinthians, "Imitate me, just as I also imitate Christ" (1 Corinthians 11:1). Paul also instructed the young pastor Timothy to be an example to other believers in word, conduct, love, spirit, faith, and purity (1 Timothy 4:12). Paul challenged the Philippians to follow his teaching and lifestyle: "The things which you learned and received and heard and saw in me, these do, and the God of peace will be with you" (Philippians 4:9).

In Romans the challenge is to "walk in the steps of the faith which our father Abraham had" (Romans 4:12). In Hebrews it is to follow in the faith and conduct of one's spiritual teachers (Hebrews 13:7). The Apostle James commands us to be "doers of the word" (James 1:22). Peter exhorts the saints to do good works among the worldly skeptics and live honorable lives above reproach (1 Peter 2:12). The elderly Apostle John reminds his spiritual children to demonstrate love through deeds of truth (1 John 3:18).

In the Old Testament, parents are commanded to diligently teach their children the Word of God and to set a godly example. Particularly, the parents were to memorize and meditate on the Scriptures and to use the Scriptures in the presence of their children during all the family affairs of eating, traveling, preparing for bed, and morning devotions (Deuteronomy 6:7). The parents' reverence for the Lord and love for the Holy Scriptures are transmitted from generation to generation, assuring the blessing of God on our offspring (Deuteronomy 6:10-11).

How does this work in practice? Daws Trotman, the great exponent of Scripture memory for his generation, insisted that the person who failed to "set the pace" in his own Scripture memory program would have little success in getting others to memorize. He gave a startling example to demonstrate this principle.

Daws had a half-dozen leaders for his boys' and girls' high school Bible clubs. Of course he insisted on a rigorous program of Scripture memory. All groups did well . . . except one. Its leader said she couldn't get her girls to memorize no matter what she tried. Daws asked her privately, "How is *your* Scripture memory program going?" You can probably guess her embarrassing answer.

God doesn't seem to bless us in areas where we are unwilling to "set the pace." This lesson was deeply imprinted on my heart during my first missionary term among the people of Communist China. One of my primary goals was to get Chinese young people to hide the Word of God in their hearts, knowing that great trials and persecutions were ahead in that country for all true believers in Jesus Christ.

Daws had already supervised the translation of the Navigator *Topical Memory System* into Chinese and had sent thousands of memory sets into China before the Communist takeover. I urged the Christians I knew there to begin memorizing Scripture and gave them their first packet of verses. It was called the "Chu Hsin Chi Yao," roughly translated "Elementary Spiritual Needs."

I felt greatly stirred at that time to deepen my own program in Scripture memory and quiet time. I encouraged my co-workers to also help set the pace. I tackled new verses in English and memorized some key verses in Chinese. We spent a great amount of time in meditation and review. This team of pacesetters helped influence about twelve hundred people to successfully memorize one packet or more of the memory program during those first months in Communist China.

When I left, the memory program was reprinted by a godly pastor. Perhaps the memory cards are still being reproduced and circulated among the thousands of saints in mainland China.

The principle of pacesetting is vital. Want to teach someone to pray? Pray together with him. Want to show someone how to witness? Go out and contact the unsaved together. Want to get somebody to memorize Scripture? Sharpen your own memory program. Want to get your children to live in purity? Check your own leisure habits. Want to make a disciple for Christ? Be one yourself.

"EACH TO HIS OWN BENT"

Spiritual reproduction does not mean turning out carbon copies. Every life is an original. The second major principle of preparing your children to be spiritual reproducers is to recognize that each has his own gifts and calling.

"Train up a child in the way he should go, and when he is old he will not depart from it" (Proverbs 22:6). Pastor Ray Stedman observes that the Hebrew idea of training "in the way he should go" could be rendered "according to his own bent." If the parent wisely trains up a child according to his own bent, then the child will go on to fulfill a productive place in the service of God.

The New Testament develops the theme of the diversity of gifts needed to serve the one Body of Christ (Romans 12, 1 Corinthians 12). Since much has been written on this theme, I will not attempt to elaborate on it here. I will move on directly to the application.

Our disciple needs to be trained, on the one hand, in the basic essentials of fruitful Christian living, and, on the other hand, according to his particular gifts and talents. Try to build on the disciple's strengths and minimize his weaknesses. Don't harp on the weaknesses; we all have them. Protect him from harm, but don't nag.

On the contrary, praise and build on those spontaneous actions and interests that show a spiritual gift or "a bent" for a certain kind of service in the overall program of God. Discovering this bent is one of the things that makes disciplemaking so exciting!

Here is the balancing factor in pacesetting. You may lead and train a young disciple in the basics of Christian living, but he may have a gift that will eventually take him far beyond you as he develops. He may have the gift of public speaking, the gift of administration, or of business, service, encouragement, or evangelism. Don't hold him back when these talents begin to rise to the surface. For each disciple is a man or woman designed by God!

A word of warning: Do not get discouraged too easily with the seemingly slow progress of your disciple. Remember how long it took you and me to win some of our early battles—and how patient God has been with us in all our tumbles and discouragements.

My language teacher taught me an interesting Chinese proverb, "Bu pa man; chih pa chan," meaning "Do not be afraid of progressing slowly; only be afraid of standing still." As the modern proverb goes, "Please be patient. God is not finished with me yet." How comforting!

Paul said, "Let us not grow weary while doing good, for in due season we shall reap if we do not lose heart" (Galatians 6:9). Our investment in other lives will pay eternal dividends far beyond our natural expectations.

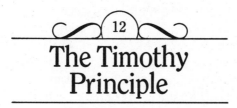

The Timothy
Principle

Dawson Trotman, a very practical man as well as a spiritual man, used "the Timothy principle" as a springboard for exhorting a fellow Christian worker to be constantly grooming someone else to take over his job. The evangelist should be grooming a younger evangelist, the choir leader an assistant, the Bible study leader the person who will take over when he leaves, and so on.

Daws carefully inspected the Navigator ministry, sometimes startling a young staff member with these unsettling words: "Where is *your* Timothy?" He wanted to know, "Who are you training to take over your job?" This is a very practical business principle as well as a great spiritual foundation for an ongoing ministry. But what is a Timothy? Where does this concept come from in Scripture?

1. *A Timothy is a spiritual child.*—"For this reason I have sent Timothy to you, who is my beloved and faithful son in the Lord" (1 Corinthians 4:17). "Paul, an apostle of Jesus Christ

. . . to Timothy, my true son in the faith" (1 Timothy 1:1-2). "You therefore, my son, be strong in the grace that is in Christ Jesus" (2 Timothy 2:1).

Every mature Christian man or woman should have a spiritual son or daughter, just as Paul served as a spiritual father to Timothy. It doesn't matter whether you led this person to the Lord or if you "adopt" him or her. Both are legitimate ways to gain spiritual children.

2. *A Timothy has a kindred spirit with his spiritual parent.*—"I have no one like-minded, who will sincerely care for your state. For all seek their own, not the things which are of Christ Jesus" (Philippians 2:20-21). "Timothy . . . who is my beloved and faithful son in the Lord . . . will remind you of my ways in Christ, as I teach everywhere in every church" (1 Corinthians 4:17). "You have carefully followed my doctrine, manner of life, purpose, faith, longsuffering, love, perseverance, persecutions, afflictions, which happened to me at Antioch, at Iconium, at Lystra" (2 Timothy 3:10-11).

Timothy was not just a spiritual child to Paul; he was a very special child. Not every physical child becomes a true believer, and not every spiritual child embraces the full vision and spirit of his spiritual parent. A Christian worker may produce many converts in his lifetime, but very few whom he can call a Timothy. A spiritual mother may influence many daughters to follow the Lord, but only a very few will probably embrace her full vision and spirit.

You pass on to your Timothy not just your knowledge of the Word, but your very heart and vision. Daws Trotman spoke of getting these principles into a person's bloodstream, for the life itself is in one's blood.

3. *A Timothy carries on the work of his spiritual parent.*— Not only is he a spiritual child, one who has a kindred spirit with the spiritual parent, but he is available to carry on the work of his spiritual parent under the parent's direction. Your

Timothy is available to help you in your ministry under your direction. This is another reason why there may be many sons and daughters, but few Timothys. Paul was able to send Timothy here and there, wherever the need was greatest:

a. To Corinth—"For this reason I have sent Timothy to you" (1 Corinthians 4:17).

b. To Philippi—"I trust in the Lord Jesus to send Timothy to you shortly" (Philippians 2:19).

c. To Athens—"Those who conducted Paul brought him to Athens; and receiving a command for Silas and Timothy to come to him with all speed, they departed" (Acts 17:15).

d. To remain in Ephesus—"As I urged you when I went into Macedonia—remain in Ephesus" (1 Timothy 1:3).

I had the rare privilege of being discipled personally by Dawson Trotman. He invited me to live in his home and invested many hours in my life. He sent me to various places: to handle the ministry assignment in the Los Angeles area, to open up a Navigator ministry in Dallas, Texas. One day he said over the telephone that he was transferring me to China. I went immediately, without reservation. If Daws, my spiritual father, felt that I could handle the assignment, then everything was okay. Never mind the 10,000 miles distance, the change of language and culture, the Communists, and all the uncertainty. Naturally, I trusted God, who had given me some verses to cling to. But also I went with the conscious knowledge of the protective umbrella of faith provided by my spiritual father.

In future years I learned that there were certain national workers whom I had trained and sheltered who would also venture out on daring exploits for God . . . if I had the faith to send them forth. This is what the work of missions is all about. The missionary carries the torch as far as he can, then passes it on to a younger disciple who will continue running, carrying the gospel light into the darkness.

In my thirty-five years on the mission field God has been

pleased to grant me many sons, a few of whom are Timothys. Over fifty Asian men have lived in my home for a year or more. Each has a special place in my heart. These fifty spiritual sons are serving God in many lands with various Christian organizations.

God commanded Moses to give "some of [his] authority" to Joshua (Numbers 27:20). And Elijah put his prophet's mantle over the shoulder of Elisha, his successor. Where is your Timothy? Who are you training to carry on your work, your Sunday school class, your Bible study, your church, your ministry? While busy serving God in your own personal ministry, don't neglect to raise up a Timothy who will carry on the task with a kindred spirit after you leave the scene. If you don't, much of your labor may be in vain.

The Key Man
Strategy

In the course of our spiritual reproduction, not everyone we work with will become a Timothy—a person whom we train to take over our particular ministry when we move on to something else. While we are in the ministry of spiritual reproduction we should develop a "key man" strategy.

The key man strategy is different from the Timothy approach. Paul used it well: "Sopater of Berea accompanied [Paul] to Asia—also Aristarchus and Secundus of the Thessalonians, and Gaius of Derbe, and Timothy, and Tychicus and Trophimus of Asia" (Acts 20:4).

The first thing to note in this passage is that, with the exception of Timothy, each man was identified with a geographical area. Paul took these men from different areas and gave them further training as they traveled with him—sort of a traveling Bible school or seminary. Then, after this short training time together, most of them presumably returned to their own place of ministry. Some represented a city: Sopater was from Berea; Aristarchus and Secundus were from Derbe. Some represented a wider territory: Tychicus and Trophimus were identified with the vast area of Asia Minor.

Our Lord Jesus chose twelve disciples to live with Him throughout His ministry. However, Jesus did not always tell people to leave their occupations and follow Him. Sometimes He sent them back to their own cities to be witnesses for Him. Such was the case of the wild man of Gadara whose mind was restored. After Jesus cast the legion of devils out of him, he begged the Lord to join the other disciples so that he, too, could be with Him. "However, Jesus did not permit him, but said to him, 'Go home to your friends, and tell them what great things the Lord has done for you, and how He has had compassion on you'" (Mark 5:19). So this man was greatly used of God to spread the gospel in his home town, for we read, "He departed and began to proclaim in Decapolis all that Jesus had done for him; and all marveled" (Mark 5:20).

We should keep in mind this pattern of allowing certain disciples to minister in their home territory. Sometimes it is appropriate to ask a person to leave his home environment to become part of a ministry team. At other times it is important to allow the new disciple to witness in his own environment. He then becomes a "key man" who can reach into a particular segment that the leader may not have the contacts to reach. However, the mature leader should continue to help each key man with instruction, encouragement, and prayer.

There are three main components of a key man strategy:

1. *Access*—A key man, who generally is a layman, has access to a particular group, school, office, neighborhood, or cultural environment. He is already accepted and established within his own group.

2. *Adaptability*—A key man is able to take the things he has learned from his spiritual leader and adapt them effectively to reach those in his own environment.

3. *Accountability*—A key man is accountable to some spiritual leader (it may not be the original one who discipled him), who will continue to instruct, encourage, and undergird his ministry.

In my own experience, I stumbled into a key man strategy out of necessity. After training me for two years in his home, Daws sent me to open a Navigator ministry in Texas in 1947. Though it was a full-time assignment, I also pursued two other major activities. I worked in my father's automobile business and I enrolled at Southern Methodist University as a business administration student. Since my time in the ministry was naturally limited, I invested precious hours in the lives of key men who did the ministry on their campuses. In one year we developed key men on six different campuses in Texas. I couldn't have done this without the key man strategy.

Similarly, I employed this key man strategy as a missionary in China under the Communists. Large Christian groups were suspect, but individual Christians were largely ignored by the Communist authorities in those early days. I quietly met with a few disciples in my home in Shanghai on a regular basis.

These men attended various colleges in Shanghai, and they contacted others who, in turn, contacted others. Upon graduation, they all moved out into other areas of China. Thus largely by working through individuals in key places, we were able to get 1200 people in fifty-three different cities to memorize the Word of God. The officials never gave this ministry any particular notice because we had no property, buildings, or any identifiable group meeting place.

When you implement the Timothy principle, you bring your spiritual children into your own ministry. This deepens your ministry, enabling you to do a more thorough job than you could if you were working alone. It also provides a more lasting ministry because your Timothy can carry on the work after you leave the scene. For example, Moses brought the

Israelites to the edge of the Promised Land, but Joshua, Moses' Timothy, took the people across the Jordan into their promised inheritance.

When you implement the key man strategy, you help your spiritual children to develop their own ministry within the context where God has placed them. This greatly broadens your influence and scope of operation, because your spiritual children have access to situations that are not open to you. This forces you to grow and broadens your own perspective, enabling you to assist them in new and challenging situations.

As we carefully implement the Timothy principle and the key man strategy, we help accomplish the Great Commission given by Jesus (Matthew 28:19-20). "Go therefore and make disciples of all the nations, baptizing them in the name of the Father and of the Son and of the Holy Spirit, teaching them to observe all things that I have commanded you; and lo, I am with you always, even to the end of the age."

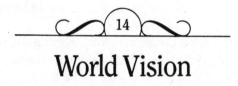

World Vision

On the eve of my departure to become the first Navigator missionary, Dawson invited me to his room for a time of prayer and commissioning. I was surprised that this man of God would invite me into his private chamber for such an occasion.

After we chatted a bit, Daws gave me instructions regarding my assignment. I feel that it was not a job description but rather a "sonship" position. In essence, Daws told me to go to China and do all that he had taught me.

Then Daws, as was his custom, gave me a verse of Scripture that was to become a keystone in my new ministry. It was Isaiah 43:19: "Behold, I will do a new thing, now it shall spring forth; shall you not know it? I will even make a road in the wilderness and rivers in the desert."

Then he put his hands on my head as I knelt before him. We prayed. I will never forget a part of that prayer: "Lord, lay on the heart of this young man what is on Your heart." As Daws prayed I wondered, "What is on the heart of God?"

Daws gave the answer as he continued to intercede for me: "Lay on his heart the field—the field of the world. Give this young man a heart for the whole world."

I said, "Amen. Yes, Lord, put on my heart a burden for the whole world. Jesus died for the *whole world*."

I have never met a man, before or since, who had such a vivid, stimulating, and practical vision for world evangelism as did Dawson Trotman. His vision was activated through spiritual reproduction.

Without such a dynamic vision, meeting with one ordinary person under mundane circumstances at an inconvenient time can seem like a small matter and a troublesome chore. There is no roar of the crowd, no awards, no applause. It is the quiet of one-to-one. Yet in that one other person lies the seed of many generations—the key to reaching the world.

THREE THINGS WE NEED TO SEE

I was sent out with a verse from Isaiah. Each of us needs three visions that Isaiah can give us for reaching the world:

1. *A vision of God*—Isaiah said, "I saw the Lord sitting on a throne, high and lifted up, and the train of His robe filled the temple" (Isaiah 6:1).

We need to sense and feel the power of God as we engage in ministry to Him. Jesus passed on His *authority* to us and commanded us to go and make disciples in every segment of society in every nation (Matthew 28:18-20, Acts 1:8). The humblest Christian, though he may be clad in rags, is clothed with the supreme authority of heaven and earth as he opens his mouth to share the truth of the Scriptures.

It is reported that John Knox of Scotland was invited to visit the queen. His friends were delighted that the queen would request a personal audience with a mere preacher, so they asked Knox to tell them what it was like to be in the presence of the great queen. Knox gave a very unexpected answer when he said, "Why should I be so impressed to meet an earthly queen when I have just spent an hour with the King of kings and Lord of lords?!"

We need a vision of God to lift us from the mundane to do service for His glory.

2. *A vision of himself*—Isaiah saw himself, and what he saw was not pretty. "Woe is me, for I am undone! Because I am a man of unclean lips, and I dwell in the midst of a people of unclean lips; for my eyes have seen the King, the LORD of hosts" (Isaiah 6:5).

The Apostle Paul reminded that bunch of reclaimed infidels who made up the membership of the Corinthian church that most of them were not from a wise, mighty, or noble heritage. He said, "God has chosen the foolish things of the world to put to shame the wise, and God has chosen the weak things of the world to put to shame the things which are mighty; and the base things of the world and the things which are despised God has chosen, and the things which are not, to bring to nothing the things that are" (1 Corinthians 1:27-28).

Isaiah saw himself in his corrupt state and cried out for cleansing and mercy. God touched his lips and made him clean. God used him, as He also used the Corinthians.

3. *A vision of the need*—Isaiah saw the need of carrying the Word of God to the people: "I heard the voice of the Lord, saying: 'Whom shall I send, and who will go for Us?" (Isaiah 6:8).

Jesus said, "Do you not say, 'There are still four months and then comes the harvest'? Behold, I say to you, lift up your eyes and look at the fields, for they are already white for harvest!" (John 4:35). The Lord told His disciples, "The harvest truly is plentiful, but the laborers are few" (Matthew 9:37). Who among God's people is ready, willing, and able to go into the harvest?

DOES SPIRITUAL REPRODUCTION REALLY WORK?

I am convinced that spiritual reproduction is an extremely effective means of carrying out the Great Commission. In 1962 my family moved to Singapore to open the Navigator work in that city-country located in the center of Asia's millions. Within a three-thousand mile radius of Singapore lies half the world's population.

A few weeks after my arrival, I decided to spend a day with the Lord claiming His promises and seeking strategy for this new ministry. The Lord impressed me with Genesis 13:17: "Arise, walk in the land through its length and its width, for I will give it to you." The context of this verse is God's promise to Abraham that his seed would multiply to bless the whole earth.

One Sunday morning soon after that I decided to spend the day in prayer and meditation as I walked across the island of Singapore. The distance from the harbor in the center of Singapore to the causeway at the other end, linking the island with Malaysia, is only sixteen miles. Sitting on a bench overlooking the world's third busiest seaport, I observed hundreds of ships bound for ports throughout the world. I asked God for the privilege of sending forth men who would likewise touch all parts of the globe. Throughout the day, as I walked from one end of the island to the other, I pleaded with God to raise up generations of people who would reach out into Asia and beyond.

Toward the end of the day, I stopped at the Kranji Memorial, a cemetery dedicated to those who had given their lives to defend Singapore from the Japanese invasion in 1942. The names of 22,000 men were engraved in stone under an inscription expressing that these men died so that others might live. The thought came to me that if thousands of soldiers were willing to die for a faroff British crown that would not last, surely there must be men here who would be willing to give their lives for Jesus Christ, a King whose Kingdom would last forever. That very afternoon I asked God for the privilege of raising up the foundations of spiritual generations.

I already had a spiritual grandson in Singapore. During my service days, I'd spent much one-to-one time with another serviceman. He acquired a teaching position in Singapore after the war and passed on what I had taught him to a teenage Singaporean named Tom Lee. Tom likewise became one of the foundations in reaching other generations.

Another key contact was Jim Chew, who had received five months of training from Navigator representative Warren Myers in Vietnam. Jim met us when we arrived in Singapore. He had already begun raising up disciples for Christ.

For eight years my wife and I gave ourselves to this great open door, meeting with individuals as God gave us the opportunity. Several Asians moved into our home in order to have more intensive ministry contact.

During the final year of overseeing the Navigator ministry in Singapore, I was given the assignment to develop a new ministry in Indonesia. My time was limited, since I spent at least a third of it in travel outside Singapore. During this final year we did not have as much program and group activity as we did normally. Instead, I spent most of my time meeting with individuals and encouraging our co-laborers also to minister one-on-one. We set goals to raise up thirty "mighty men" (1 Chronicles 11:11) and thirty "godly girls" (Proverbs 31) during the year. The main qualification to become a mighty man or godly woman was to *reproduce to the third generation* on a one-on-one basis. In other words, the challenge was to become a spiritual grandparent. There were other stipulations such as meeting weekly with yet another disciple. Each disciple was checked for consistency in quiet time, Scripture memory, and personal Bible study (all the disciplines taught in Chapters 4 and 5 of this book). Finally, each disciple was to have at least one responsibility in his or her local church.

I met individually with six men at scheduled weekly times whenever I was in the country. Each of these men met individually with others. My wife met with several women in the same way. These men and women disciples all reproduced to the third generation; two of them reproduced to the fourth. Later, one numbered his spiritual descendants to the fifth generation. By God's grace, at the end of the year we qualified thirty-seven "godly girls" and thirty-four "mighty men."

The excitement generated by the testimony of these people encouraged many others to do a similar type of work. And so the individual discipleship formula spread throughout the city. We did not manage all this, but merely had a part in stimulating it.

Fifteen years later on a recent trip to Singapore, I read in the newspaper that a survey revealed that half of the educated English-speaking people in Singapore were now Christians. Formerly, the percentage of Christians was less then ten percent. Something had happened in the course of two decades. With the work of many groups committed to discipleship, such as Youth for Christ, Campus Crusade for Christ, Scripture Union, InterVarsity, and mainline churches—the Methodists, Brethren, Baptists, Presbyterians, Assembly of God, etc.—the complexion of the city was changed through individuals who shared their faith and experience with other individuals.

We started some of these chains of reproduction, but we simply could not control the momentum. The one-on-one work exploded in all directions. Other Christian groups and denominations caught on to the idea and used it with their own modifications and standards. Singapore was an ideal spot for carrying out spiritual reproduction because the country was so small and tightly knit that the contacts could not move out of reach. One had no excuses for not keeping in touch. One's spiritual babe would either reproduce or falter before your eyes.

Today Singapore is influencing all of Asia, and has sent

forth disciplemakers into the fields of India, Thailand, Japan, Hong Kong, mainland China, and other countries. Faithful disciples will reach others, who will reach even others. Spiritual reproduction is the vital link in carrying out the Great Commission.

How do you implement the lessons from this book? Remember, the harvest is not just overseas. The mission field is right outside your own door—at least, the first step. First is your local area; next is your general area; *then* we are called "to the end of the earth" (Acts 1:8).

But the time to get started is today! The seed of the gospel is in you. Win someone to Christ. Help that new babe grow. Begin reproducing yourself in him. Share with him the principles of Christ-centered living. Instill world vision in him. You teach him to reproduce himself. Then the chain of spiritual reproduction will continue around the world.

Appendix

**A SUGGESTED TEACHING PLAN
BASED ON THE WHEEL**

Stage A—BASIC COMMITMENT

    Phase 1: *Hub of the Wheel—Salvation*
          Review the plan of salvation, using the
          Bridge.

    Phase 2: *Hub of the Wheel—Assurance of Salvation*
          (Christ lives in us)
          Teach assurance of salvation, using the
          Beginning with Christ memory packet for
          newborn Christians.

    Phase 3: *The Wheel Illustration*
          Present an overall view of the basics of the
          Christian life, using the Wheel.

    Phase 4: *Rim of the Wheel—The Obedient Christian*
          Teach the importance of commitment to
          Lordship, allowing Jesus to control every

area of our lives (Romans 12:1-2), and the importance of obedience to all portions of the Word of God. Such commitment and obedience is proof of our love for Jesus in obedience to His Word (John 14:15,21).

Stage B—DISCIPLINE IN THE WORD
Phase 5: *The Word Spoke of the Wheel*
Magnify the Word spoke of the Wheel illustration by explaining the Hand illustration, which shows five ways someone can get a good grasp on the Word: hearing, reading, studying, memorizing, and meditating (see Chapter 4).

Phase 6: *The Word Spoke—Emphasis on Reading*
Teach the importance of daily Bible reading, using the Hand illustration. Help the disciple incorporate this emphasis in his life in a daily quiet time.

Phase 7: *The Word Spoke—Emphasis on Bible Study*
Teach the disciple how to do a personal Bible study, using the Hand illustration and the five elements of personal Bible study:
1. Original investigation
2. Regular and systematic
3. Written reproduction
4. Personal application
5. Easily passed on.

Phase 8: *The Word Spoke—Emphasis on Scripture Memory*
Teach the benefits of Scripture memory and the importance of embarking on a lifetime program of memorizing Scripture, using the Hand illustration.

Stage C—PRAYER AND FELLOWSHIP

Phase 9: *The Prayer Spoke of the Wheel—Quiet Time*
Teach the importance of quiet time habits: person, period, place, and plan (see Chapter 4).

Phase 10: *The Prayer Spoke of the Wheel—The Prayer Hand*
Teach the elements of the Prayer Hand
1. Confession
2. Thanksgiving
3. Intercession
4. Petition
5. Praise.

Phase 11: *The Fellowship Spoke of the Wheel—Local Fellowship*
Teach the importance of attending church and being linked with vital fellowship (Hebrews 10:25, 1 John 1:3).

Phase 12: *The Fellowship Spoke of the Wheel—Service to the Body*
Teach the importance of being linked with the Body of Christ in loving service.

Stage D—OUTREACH

Phase 13: *The Witness Spoke of the Wheel—The Principles of Witnessing*
Teach the principles of witnessing by life and words:
1. Walk (godly life)
2. Winsome (friendship)
3. Witness (testimony)
4. Word (the gospel)
5. Will you? (decision).

Phase 14: *The Witness Spoke of the Wheel—*

Personal Testimony
Teach the disciple how to give a personal testimony.

Phase 15: *The Witness Spoke of the Wheel—Spiritual Reproduction*
Teach the disciple the principles of spiritual reproduction (John 15:16).

Phase 16: *The Witness Spoke of the Wheel—Follow-up*
Teach the disciple how to follow up on his new convert.

Stage E—SPIRITUAL REPRODUCTION
Continue to train the new disciple to work with another follower of Christ.

The following syllabus is a suggested one-on-one program incorporating all materials, assignments, weekly projects, and check-ups of this teaching plan.

A SUGGESTED SYLLABUS

(A weekly, one-on-one discipling guide)

Stage A—BASIC COMMITMENT
Phase 1: *Salvation*
Teaching—Review God's plan of salvation (the Bridge illustration).
New material—Give the disciple the *Beginning with Christ* memory booklet.
Assignment—Assign at least two verses to memorize from *Beginning with Christ*.
Project—Ask the disciple to explain the Bridge illustration to someone else, either a *Christian* or a nonChristian.

Phase 2: *Assurances*

Check-up—Ask the disciple to quote his memory verses and to explain the Bridge illustration.

Teaching—Teach the disciple the assurances given in the *Beginning with Christ* booklet.

New material—Give the first lesson of a question-answer Bible study (*Your Decision* by Lorne Sanny and *Lessons on Assurance* by Daws Trotman, both published by NavPress, are recommended).

Assignment—Ask the disciple to memorize new verses and to prepare the first lesson of Bible study.

Project—Challenge the disciple to begin a daily quiet time of personal devotions.

Phase 3: *The Wheel*

Check-up—Ask the disciple to quote his memory verses, turn in his Bible study, and comment on his quiet time.

Teaching—Present the Wheel illustration in order to teach the basics of Christian discipleship.

New material—Present notebook materials (see Chapter 4).

Assignment—Assign new memory verses (When *Beginning with Christ* verses are complete, continue with *Going on with Christ,* the *Topical Memory System,* or some other memorization program and a second lesson of Bible study).

Project—Encourage the disciple to begin to use the prayer pages of the notebook materials.

Phase 4: *Obedience*

Check-up—Ask the disciple to quote his memory verses, hand in his second lesson of Bible study, and comment on his use of the prayer pages.

Review—Ask the disciple to present the Wheel in his own words.

Teaching—Major on rim of the Wheel as you teach the disciple about the submissive, obedient Christian:

1. Romans 12:1-2—Submission to Christ as Lord over every area of our lives.
2. John 14:15,21—The proof of our love of God is our obedience to His Word.

New material—Explain the use of the quiet time notebook page.

Assignment—Assign new memory verses and a third lesson of Bible study.

Project—Ask the disciple to list the areas of his life in which Christ must have control.

Stage B—DISCIPLINE

Phase 5: *Hand—Overview*

Check-up—Ask the disciple to quote his memory verses, hand in his third lesson of Bible study, and report on his quiet time.

Review—Ask the disciple to comment on the meaning of a Lordship commitment.

Teaching—Present five ways to grasp the Word of God, using the Hand illustration.

New material—Present notebook page on the hand.

Assignment—Continue with an assignment on Scripture memory and the fourth lesson

of Bible study, and remind the disciple to
keep up his quiet time.

Project—Ask the disciple to learn to explain
the Hand illustration.

Phase 6: *The Hand—Reading*

Check-up—Ask the disciple to quote his
memory verses, hand in his Bible study lesson, and report on his quiet time.

Review—Ask the disciple to present the
Hand illustration.

Teaching—Using the Hand reading finger,
emphasize the importance of regular reading
of the Word (Deuteronomy 17:18-19, Nehe-
miah 8:8, 1 Timothy 4:13).

Assignment—Continue with an assignment
on Scripture memory, Bible study, and quiet
time. Also, ask the disciple to begin reading a
chapter a day in the Bible.

Project—Work out together with the disciple
a schedule for his regular Bible reading.

Phase 7: *The Hand—Bible Study*

Check-up—Ask the disciple to quote his
memory verses, hand in his Bible study (he
should have completed the *Lessons on Assurance* or five lessons of some other question-
answer Bible study by now), and report on
his prayer time and daily Bible reading.

Teaching—Emphasize the Bible study finger
of the Hand. Teach the disciple the five elements of personal Bible study:

1. Original investigation
2. Regular and systematic
3. Written reproduction
4. Personal application

5. Easily passed on.

New material—introduce Point Blank, a simple personal Bible study (see Chapter 5).

Project—Ask the disciple to do an original Bible study, using Point Blank, on an assigned portion of Scripture (example in Chapter 5).

Assignment—Continue with an assignment consisting of memory verses, quiet time, Bible reading, and original Bible study.

Phase 8: *The Hand—Scripture memory*

Check-up—Check on memory verses, Bible reading, and quiet time.

Review—Ask the disciple to explain the principles of Bible study, and discuss his first original Bible study.

Teaching—Teach the benefits of Scripture memory (see Chapter 5).

New material—Present the disciple with the memory page for his notebook.

Assignment—Assign new memory verses, a second personal Bible study, quiet time, and Bible reading.

Project—Ask the disciple to list references from his current memory program on the memory page in his notebook.

Stage C—PERSONAL GROWTH

Phase 9: *Quiet Time Habits*

Check-up—Check on memory verses, Bible study, Bible reading, and quiet time.

Review—Review together the benefits of Scripture memory.

Teaching—Teach the disciple the importance

of quiet time habits (see Chapter 4), emphasizing the elements of person, period, place,
and plan.

Assignment—Assign memory verses, Bible
study, and Bible reading.

Project—Ask the disciple to determine the
minimum period for a regular, consistent
quiet time.

Phase 10: *The Hand of Prayer*

Check-up—Check on memory verses, Bible
reading, Bible study, and quiet time.

Review—Discuss the problems of having a
regular quiet time.

Teaching—Teach the disciple the principles
of the Hand of Prayer:

1. Confession (Psalm 66:18, 1 John 1:9)
2. Thanksgiving (1 Thessalonians 5:18,
   Ephesians 5:20)
3. Intercession (1 Thessalonians 1:1-2, Colossians 4:3)
4. Petition (Matthew 21:22, 1 John 5:14-15)
5. Praise (Psalm 107:8,15,21,31, Acts 16:25).

Assignment—Assign memory verses, Bible
reading, Bible study, and quiet time.

New material—Introduce the intercessory
prayer sheet to the disciple for his notebook.

Project—Ask the disciple to develop an
intercessory prayer list for Monday through
Sunday in his notebook (see the example in
Chapter 4).

Phase 11: *Fellowship—Being linked with the Body of
Christ*

Check-up—Check on memory verses, Bible
reading, Bible study, and quiet time.

Review—Ask the disciple to present the Hand of Prayer and discuss the intercessory prayer list.

Teaching—Teach the disciple the importance of attending church and being linked with a vital Christian fellowship (Hebrews 10:25, 1 John 1:3).

New material—Introduce the notebook page for taking notes on sermons.

Assignment—Continue in the basics.

Project—Ask the disciple to use the notebook page to take notes on his pastor's sermon this week.

Phase 12: *Fellowship—Serving the Body of Christ*

Check-up—Go through the basic check-up.

Review—Allow the disciple to review his pastor's sermon.

Teaching—Teach about the spiritual gifts and how they can best serve the Body of Christ (Romans 12).

Assignment—Continue in the basics.

Project—Ask the disciple to think of one way that he can serve the Body of Christ.

Stage D—OUTREACH

Phase 13: *Witnessing*

Check-up—Check up on the basics and on personal victory over sin.

Review—Give the disciple an opportunity to explain how he can serve the Body of Christ.

Teaching—Teach the disciple how to witness through his life and words:

1. Walk (godly life)—Ephesians 4:1, 5:15-16

2. Winsome (friendship)—John 4:9, Proverbs 18:24
3. Witness (testimony)—Acts 26:1-29
4. Word (the gospel)—1 Corinthians 15:1-4
5. Will you? (decision)—Acts 28:23-24.

Assignment—Continue in the basic assignments.

Project—Challenge the disciple to make one new nonChristian friend.

Phase 14: *How to Give a Personal Testimony*

Check-up—Check on the disciple's basic progress. Does he have joy and peace?

Review—Discuss with the disciple how to make friends with nonChristians while remaining separate from the world.

Teaching—Teach the disciple how to give his personal testimony (Acts 26) of his life in four minutes:

1. His life before salvation (one minute)
2. Details on how he became a Christian (two minutes)
3. How he changed (one minute).

Assignment—Continue in the basic assignments.

Project—Ask the disciple to write out his personal testimony.

Phase 15: *Reproduction*

Check-up—Go over the basics.

Review—Allow the disciple to give his written personal testimony verbally.

Teaching—Teach the disciple the principles of spiritual reproduction (John 15:16).

Assignment—Continue in the basics.

Project—As an effort toward spiritual repro-

duction, ask the disciple to share his testimony and/or the Bridge illustration this
week with someone, asking that person if he
wants to make a salvation decision.

Phase 16: *Follow-up*
Check-up—Check the basic progress in the
disciple's life.
Review—Discuss your disciple's attempt to
reproduce.
Teaching—If your disciple was successful,
teach him how to follow up on his new disciple (see the spiritual parenthood concepts
in 1 Thessalonians 2:1-12).
Project—Challenge your disciple to begin to
work with this new believer, teaching him
what he himself has been taught in this
program.

Stage E—SPIRITUAL REPRODUCTION
Continue to train your disciple in his life and ministry
of working with another follower of Christ.

NAVIGATOR DISCIPLESHIP MATERIALS

BIBLE STUDY MATERIALS
Design for Discipleship—7-book Bible study series with
leader's guide
Gospel of John Bible Study—4-part study available through
Training Evangelistic Leadership, 1306 Tulane, Denton,
TX 76201 (not available through NavPress)
Navigator Bible Studies Handbook—includes ABC, advanced
ABC, and Search the Scriptures
Studies in Christian Living—9-book Bible study series with
leader's guide

Think It Through—follow-up Bible study by George Howard

FOLLOW-UP TOOLS AND
PERSONAL GROWTH MATERIALS
Beginning with Christ—booklet on five key assurances
Lessons on Assurance—companion Bible study for *Beginning with Christ*
Going on with Christ—booklet on eight key Scripture verses
Lessons on Christian Living—companion Bible study for *Going on with Christ*
Essentials of New Life—book for young Christians by Francis Cosgrove
Essentials of Discipleship—book on the basics of discipleship by Cosgrove
Personal Growth Notebook Set—includes the Wheel, the Hand, and Bible Reading Plan and Chart
Your Decision—study booklet on the Gospel of John by Lorne Sanny
Appointment with God—2-book set on the quiet time discipline

SCRIPTURE MEMORY TOOLS
Topical Memory System—complete Scripture memory system
Scripture Memory Packs—each of these eight topical packs contains 36 key passages

DISCIPLESHIP MATERIALS
The Lost Art of Disciple Making—book of disciplemaking principles by LeRoy Eims
Multiplying Disciples—book on spiritual multiplication by Waylon Moore
Jesus Christ, Disciplemaker—book on Jesus' techniques of making disciples by Bill Hull
Born to Reproduce—booklet on the principles of spiritual

reproduction by Dawson Trotman

The Need of the Hour—booklet on reaching the world for
   Christ by Trotman

Materials available through NavPress, P.O. Box 6000, Colorado Springs, CO 80934